HOW TO IGNITE YOUR INNER STRENGTH

To Expand and Manifest Your Personal Essence

Dominique Lamy

How to Ignite Your Inner Strength
www.IgniteYourInnerStrengthCoach.com

Copyright © 2017 Dominique Lamy

ISBN: 978-1-77277-183-1

All rights reserved. No portion of this book may be reproduced mechanically, electronically, or by any other means, including photocopying, without permission of the publisher or author except in the case of brief quotations embodied in critical articles and reviews. It is illegal to copy this book, post it to a website, or distribute it by any other means without permission from the publisher or author.

Limits of Liability and Disclaimer of Warranty
The author and publisher shall not be liable for your misuse of the enclosed material. This book is strictly for informational and educational purposes only.

Warning – Disclaimer
The purpose of this book is to educate and entertain. The author and/or publisher do not guarantee that anyone following these techniques, suggestions, tips, ideas, or strategies will become successful. The author and/or publisher shall have neither liability nor responsibility to anyone with respect to any loss or damage caused, or alleged to be caused, directly or indirectly by the information contained in this book.

Publisher
10-10-10 Publishing
Markham, ON
Canada

Printed in Canada and the United States of America

Table of Contents

Dedication	VII
Acknowledgments	IX
Preface	XI
Foreword	XIII

Chapter 1   1
FROM SABOTAGE TO SUCCESS
Starting My Journey   8
Where I Was   9
Where I Am Now   10
So, Why Write a Book?   11

Chapter 2   13
MY QUEST FOR FREEDOM
First, Love Yourself   14
Accept Others For Who They Are   17
Behind-the-Scenes   18
Expectations   19
You Deserve the Best!   23
Be Your Own Best Friend   24
Have Forgiveness   26
What's Holding You Back?   30
Jump Into Your Greatness   31
Becoming a Leader   31

Chapter 3   35
EMBRACE THE CHALLENGE
Transcend Old Wounds   36
Accept Who You Are   37
Conquer Thyself   39

Be Passionate	39
Have Commitment	41
Take Responsibility	41
Think Before You Choose	42
It's What's Under the Tip of the Iceberg That Counts	45
Surround Yourself with Success	46

Chapter 4 — 47
GIVE YOURSELF A CHANCE

The Wounded Child	48
The Seasons	51
Reward Yourself	54
Establish Boundaries	56
Play Hard	58
Create Your Own Balance	58

Chapter 5 — 61
CHANGE YOUR HABITS, TRANSFORM YOUR LIFE

Stay Out of Your Comfort Zone	62
Go the Extra Mile	63
Stop Pleasing Others	67
Don't Try to Change Other People	69
Change Your Mindset	70
Let Go of the Story	71
Stand Up and Speak	72

Chapter 6 — 75
STOP LYING TO YOURSELF

Attitude and Personality	77
The Four Agreements	79
The Turning Point	80
Respect Others	81
The Seven Principles of Acknowledgment	83
Be True to Yourself	83
Walk the Talk	84

Chapter 7
WHO DO YOU SEE IN THE MIRROR?   87

Roots   87
Keep Learning   89
Do You Have a Vision?   91
Courage and Sacrifice   92
There Are No Short Cuts   93
Build the New YOU   95
Be Your Own Leader   96

Chapter 8
CHOOSE TO WIN   99

Find Your Vehicle   102
Decide and Commit   103
Be Authentic   105
Do Whatever It Takes   106
Move On   107
Stick to It   107

Chapter 9
LIVE YOUR MISSION   111

Find Your Niche   113
Be of Service   115
Create Your Tools   116
Utilize Your Gift   117
Brand Yourself   119
Spread It to the World   120

Chapter 10
THE REAL CONNECTION   123

LOVE, the Acronym*   125
Follow Your Heart   125
My Body, My Temple   127

Chapter 11 129
BEING MENTORED
The Meaning of MENTOR* 130
Raise the Bar* 131
My Mentors and Teachers 133
My First Inspirations in Life 133
Napoleon Hill and My Mentors 135

Chapter 12 137
CONCLUSION
How Can I Help You? 139
Suggested Reading 141
Testimonials 143

*Free bonus to be obtained on the website
www.IgniteYourInnerStrengthCoach.com

Dedication

*To the memory of my father and, in gratitude,
to my mentors who continue to inspire me.*

*This book is for all the silenced voices
who need our help in speaking up.*

Acknowledgments

Special thanks;

To Michel Desjardins and Mélanie Gagnon, who gave me this "once in a lifetime" pivotal opportunity.

Also to Francine Turcot, a person I consider a real gift and an angel in my life; she has helped me to surrender and gain serenity of my soul during tremendous chaos.

In gratitude to Raymond Aaron, my co-author.

I'd like to express my gratefulness to you, the reader, without who it wouldn't be possible to share what I have learned.

In addition, thanks to;

My photographer Gérard Leduc.

Clayton Bye, The Napoleon Hill Foundation, Christelle Robert, Shane & Josie Morand, Holton & Earlene Buggs, Bernie & Adeline Chua, Jean-Noël Sirois & Ginette Bienvenue, Marianne Noad, Rhonda & Steve Martin, Ivan & Elaina Sisco, Rod Smith, John and Blanca Sachtouras, The Nielsen Family, Jose Ardon, and all others in the Diamondship.

Monica Dokupil, Annick Desmarais & Éric Henri, Dean Martin, Marie-Luce Frenette, Rudolph Isidore & Sukaina Pierre-Louis, Alain Thériault, Kristine Marsolais, Julie Labrosse, Marie-Claude Sabourin, Sylvie Lefebvre, Isabelle Kieffer.

TMI community, Marcia Wieder, Robert Riopel, T. Harv Eker, New Peaks Family, Adam Markel, Caroline Wong.

How To Ignite Your Inner Strength

Jeanne Bélanger, Bernadette Lefebvre, Monique Larue (my mom).

There are collaborations with some people who are meant to cross your path, and when they do, they really help you to propel yourself at a higher state of being. Miriam Cohen, my editor, with whom I have had the huge privilege of walking closely on this part of my journey, is one of them. She is, for me, a pure delight of happiness and she has given me so much support to reach more deeply within myself to share my story. At the same time, as the partnership went on, Miriam taught me how to bridge thoughts and move them around a little bit until... BOOM. Here it is! The perfect alignment of words takes place, and she has made my stress disappear so I may continue to go on, and on.

Miriam, people don't realize the importance of your work behind MY scene, as you are patiently being of service, benevolently listening and providing an accurate presence. You have helped me with your intelligence and wise reflections, without judging, mastering your role as a wonderful editor. I now understand what it means to really work the whole process together, as you hold my hand and respect my writing and my voice, the way I intend to communicate more clearly with the readers. How beneficial it has been to team up with you Miriam. You are for me, even as we haven't met in person, a friend. You humbly know how to step back, exactly when to comment, what and how to reformulate for the reader to better understand my point of who I am. You are a strong, meaningful, beautiful, and sensitive woman who has brought us to create this artwork, for which I am really grateful. This is when we may say the rubber hits the road, right? Blessings to you Miriam Cohen.

Preface

No one's path in life is a straight line to success. The highs energize us, and the lows teach us valuable lessons that allow us to better meet the challenges that lie ahead. Some lucky souls have a destination in mind from the beginning of their journey, but most trudge on more than they run. And, then, there are people whose path is particularly difficult, full of more and deeper lows, as well as demoralizing events that make them question their own worth and perfect defense mechanisms that don't always serve them well.

How glorious are the rare few who rise from the ashes of their past! Even more so are the ones who then share what they have learned and the actions they have taken to turn their lives around in the hope that they can help others to manifest success in both their personal and business lives. Dominique Lamy is such a person. From the moment I met her in one of my workshops, I knew she had an empowering message that had to be shared. Revealing even the most intimate lows of her life and then laying out the steps she took to heal within and move on to a more joyous place is proof positive that you can do the same.

In this book, Dominique shares many of the tools she's acquired through years of working with renowned coaches and attending workshops and programs. An avid reader and seeker of knowledge, she provides a unique perspective on integrating various self-healing and growth techniques that will help you reignite your passion and drive, manifest the things you most want in life, and develop a way of thinking that will bring you joy and prosperity.

I am proud to play a part in bringing this remarkable woman's story to the world. Dominique will inspire you as few others can.

Raymond Aaron
New York Times Bestselling Author

Foreword

You are about to read an honest, from-the-heart account of how to change your life and claim your happiness and success. Dominique Lamy will inspire you to dig deeper and fly higher than you might have imagined possible. Her passion for life and strong commitment to growing on a personal and spiritual level is contagious. Without a shadow of a doubt, I can promise you that Dominique will touch your heart as she is a courageous warrior who has worked tirelessly to remove self-imposed barriers and limiting beliefs.

Almost everyone has at least some emotional scars, whether from having over critical parents or a romance that ended badly. Some scars run far deeper than that but, it's not the hurt that matters, it's what you do about it. As someone who has studied and worked with various philosophies of self-healing and growth, I have seen even the most powerful and famous of people hold themselves back from being truly happy.

If you have ever said or done something in the heat of the moment and regretted it afterward, it may be that you were unconsciously over-reacting based on past trauma or upset. Emotional wounds that haven't healed can cloud your judgment or cause you to misinterpret someone else's words and actions. The problem is, carrying emotional baggage throughout your life can lead you to self-sabotage and low self-esteem. So many people stop themselves from achieving the relationships and success they want and deserve without realizing that's what they are doing.

Dominique's capacity to reveal her most intimate feelings and her decision to share the tools she has used to increase her confidence and overcome self-sabotaging behavior may surprise you... but not me. As a student of The Meaning Institute, Dominique has grown massively by putting all her heart, energy, and enthusiasm into her evolution.

During the year we have worked together she has also become my teacher for expressing emotion on every level.

Dominique is now ready to inspire and entertain you like no other first-time author can. She knows how to create a powerful and positive impact with complete authenticity. Her book will help you thicken your skin and soften your heart. Be prepared to be amazed by her story of finding the way out of the shadows and into the light.

Marcia Wieder
CEO, Dream University®
Founder, The Meaning Institute
Best-selling Author of multiple books

Chapter 1

From Sabotage to Success

"Our deepest fear is not that we are inadequate. Our deepest fear is that we are powerful beyond measure. It is our light, not our darkness that most frightens us. We ask ourselves, 'Who am I to be brilliant, gorgeous, talented, fabulous?' Actually, who are you not to be? You are a child of God. Your playing small does not serve the world. There is nothing enlightened about shrinking so that other people won't feel insecure around you. We are all meant to shine, as children do. We were born to make manifest the glory of God that is within us. It's not just in some of us; it's in everyone. And as we let our own light shine, we unconsciously give other people permission to do the same. As we are liberated from our own fear, our presence automatically liberates others."
— **Marianne Williamson**

The first time I read this quote, I broke into tears because the depth of this message hit me at the deepest core of my soul. It has been on my wall for years, and I read it endlessly to manifest this pure light and break through to unleash my personal essence.

This book is about my personal experiences, and it is meant to share my journey and growth with you. I don't pretend to have all the answers, but I have learned and changed so much in the last ten years that I am ready to help others by using the details of my own story to show what's possible when you dare to walk on a new path.

The moment I decided to "jump into my greatness" was when I became aware that my old ways weren't working and that I had to change. One of the biggest insights I had during my journey was that I should and could let go of the need to be right all the time, (even when I was right...ha, ha, ha). Doing battle with others more often than not wasn't working. I realized that fighting or constant arguing isn't necessary to achieve a winning point of view. I can simply do things my way, accepting that others may not do as I do since they may not be on the same path or interpret things as I do. Everything is perfect if I choose to see it that way.

What do I mean by "jump into my greatness"? As you will see this phrase quite a few times in this book, I want to explain here, at the very beginning, why it is something so very meaningful to me. Les Brown, who is inspiring to me, always ends with "you have greatness." I interpret this to mean that we are powerful beyond limitation and we have to stop dimming our real nature.

We go through lots of things in life thinking, oh well, that's nothing; no big deal. No, we are greater than we think we are and should not discount what we are capable of. For me, jumping into my greatness is being aware of that part inside of me that is aligned with how I can make a difference, be wiser and use the wisdom of an accurate consciousness to stop the weak part of me, so I don't go around walking as if asleep.

I believe in a bigger plan. We all have different patterns in our lives, and we are put in places and situations where we can learn the lessons we are supposed to learn. When we repeat these patterns, it's because the universe continues to send us other, but similar, situations so we may identify and deal with the things and behaviours with which we struggle. Have you noticed this in your own life?

Each of us has a "switch" which, when pushed, opens the Pandora's box and, boom, there we are again. If we don't learn the lesson the first, second or even the third time, the universe will keep giving us what may be bigger opportunities in the name of growth. For the most part, those circumstances stop occurring once we master the whole concept of recurrent situation although, every once in a while, we are tested again just to see if we really have learned what we needed to.

We often hear it said that we are never given more than we can handle. It's true. What do you see when you look backward in time? Here's what I see: circumstances and the way I looked at the world led me to a point where I was shut down, quite often in survival mode, hiding behind imaginary walls I had built to keep me safe. I came out on the other side of my wall with the courage and power to take on all comers. Clearly, The Big Plan is so perfectly designed!

I studied the principles of Napoleon Hill and changed my life. Hill's principles have helped me look at the events that happened to me in a different way. I now understand you should never have guilt for what other people do to you (I explain in full during later chapters). This book originated from that mindset, and from being heartfelt instead of speaking with a general lack of truthfulness. The people who treated me badly have no idea of the depth of pain from which I have come and the power I have gained from it. Today, I'm 52 and an entrepreneur who wants to help people understand that they can do anything and come from anywhere, just like I did.

Now, I invite you to witness the start of my journey. We begin by going back to the 2nd of May, 2006. It was my wedding anniversary, and it proved one of those days that change your life forever. Two totally unrelated events happened, neither of which I could have anticipated. Or, perhaps I should say, I had no warning about either of them.

I received a letter from my father, who was visiting Paris at the time. Among his many hobbies, he was a bibliophile and lover of the arts. He basically thought those fields of endeavour were wonderful and important, and his passion for them took up a huge part of his life. Yet, curiously, he had never been supportive of my choice to be an actress, a career I embarked on, first as a dilettante at the age of 17 and then professionally once I graduated from the Conservatory of dramatic art of Montreal at the age of 26. Actually, neither of my parents thought I should be an actress; they wanted me to do something more serious, useful and financially rewarding. I had always craved their support, and it was a great disappointment to me that it was not given.

In his letter, my father said that he had heard an interview with an actress, during which she talked about how her father often reminded her of the importance of the job she was doing and the essential role of theatre in our society. It was after hearing that interview, my father wrote, that he realized he had come a little late to letting me know how proud he was of me. Also, he wanted to let me know that he knew how hard it was to make a living acting and that I had succeeded at it in some ways. This acknowledgement was so unexpected that I melted into tears. It had taken until I was 41 for my father to realize how important my career was. Then, he ended his letter with these words: "Greetings to Miguel. I often think of you two. I wish both of you the success of happiness."

As if that letter wasn't enough of a surprise, later in the day, Miguel told me he was leaving. Our marriage was over. My heart split into a thousand pieces, and I broke. I fell apart. There is no other way to say it. The love of my life, my handsome Cuban husband, the man I had sponsored and waited for, was leaving. We had been a couple but living apart for two and a half years, and then had been living together in Quebec, for only a year. But, I really thought that, together, we could handle everything.

During the four years we had been a couple, we had built a powerful relationship of support for each other, and that had given me the opportunity to greatly heal from a past sexual abuse experience that started when I was 17 and didn't end until I was 30. Plus, being with Miguel was the first time I could share my confidences with someone since I had had another sad and destroying experience, that of being raped in my own apartment just three years before I met Miguel. And, this day – our wedding anniversary – was the end of my love story with this man for whom I had opened my heart.

I am telling you these details so you can understand where I was in my life. I was going through the consequences of me having been in an abusive relationship; the aggression I felt inside me had not been completely healed. Our first years together were beautiful, but we were back in my real world, far from the beaches and Miguel's own culture. I was expecting him to give me all the love on earth that I could possibly bear, given the hidden part of me that housed my innermost fears and feelings. That is what really led us to a separation.

My self-recovery was just beginning. The shame and self-destructive pattern I continued to live out as a wounded woman was inevitable in some ways. I had helped create and nurture a toxic environment for myself and others because my viewpoint was coloured by so many disrespectful relationships. But, Miguel wasn't disrespectful; he was in another fight – one for himself, the one, the missionary man. So, loving him and losing him cost me a lot emotionally.

The fact that both things occurred on the same day shook me to my core. I started on a journey that day that continues still, but I have reached a point where my experiences may help other people understand how we participate in creating unhappiness, drama, and tragedy at some level. I definitely played a part in manifesting those things in my own life.

After some time, I started to pull myself together, and I thought *What is wrong with me? Why had I been so insecure in my relationship? Why did I bully my husband when he was the one who needed support? Did I do these things so this man who loved me would leave? Why didn't he fight harder for me?* I had expected romance, but had become a teacher of so many things: showing him how to find a job, how to get his equivalency degree for welding so he could get a better job, how to drive a car, how to live outside of a tight-knit community, how to cook, how to clean his clothes, and more. I became impatient because I needed a man to support me as well. I was making Miguel feel that everything he was doing was wrong. I didn't realize how important my support was because he was the one who was far from everyone he loved, including his daughter, other close family, and his extended family. He was unrooted.

I realized that I was doing the same thing to him that I did to myself – nothing was ever good enough. Of course, Miguel was shutting down, and I knew I was the reason! I had to change – he didn't deserve what I was doing to him So, I helped him find an apartment and move. I was heartbroken. My reactions to his behaviour were, in large part, related to culture shock. I couldn't live as a Cuban wife who did everything for her husband. And, I needed to be in charge of my career and the work I was doing as one of the administrators on the Board of Directors of my union. I knew I had been wrong. I felt guilty but didn't know how to change. And, I thought, *Why can't I become successful? Why can't I be happy and feel free?*

Then, I attended a three-day seminar created by T. Harv Eker, and my eyes started to open. I decided that I had to look at myself, not in a deprecating way; not to just criticize or feel sorry for myself. I wanted my life to be better and fuller, and to do that I needed to understand why, despite all my hard work and dedication, things were not going my way. In this book, you will see how I learned new ways to stop judging myself – and others – with benevolence. Being kind instead of self-criticizing allows us to embrace the dark side of our own personality and work to change the things that are keeping us from being happy and successful. When we judge someone else, we don't acknowledge our own weaknesses, and focusing on ourselves is what we must all do if we are to be free.

During my journey, I learned how much of everything in our current life always goes back to our roots. Our parents, the places we come from, and the things that happened to us in school, as well as the education we received there, have a profound effect on the people we become. I know that even as a young child, these people and situations instilled in me beliefs, patterns and a set of fears and insecurities that had to be discovered and confronted somehow if I was going to flourish in the world. I suspect this is true for almost all people. Today, I approach my past experiences quite differently, with new and wiser eyes. I have perspective, and I know that people, most notably my parents, acted out of good intentions and the best way they could.

However, we know that how you educate your children has a huge impact on their self- confidence. I believe that my parents' generation, and their parents' generation before them, didn't learn how to express their feelings. That resulted in a lot of non-verbal communication which could be misinterpreted. It led me to "fill in the blanks" without knowing exactly what my parents and grandparents actually meant (because they didn't really express what they were feeling). I think that my hypersensitivity affected how I interpreted non-verbal cues and, so, I started to act out based on what I perceived my parents felt and what others might want when they didn't say it. Even as a child, I thought it was my responsibility to understand how I felt and to figure out how to express those feelings, even when the words that came out weren't accurate.

Since I was young, I was shown how or asked to be quiet, but I challenged the adults so I could be heard. I remember a moment (because they recorded me), when my father laughed at and made fun of me as I said "NO" to being asked to sing when I didn't want to. He continued to remind me of this story and to imitate me saying no when, on different occasions, I was being asked to do something that I didn't want to do. My brother continued this funny but confrontational way of imitating or playing me. I remember asking them to stop, but they often continued until I reached my breaking point and started to scream (as a way expressing myself), *"Stop, NOOOOO."* In response, they intensified their mocking of me. In many situations I ended up crying and screaming.

At some point, you couldn't stop me from expressing my feelings. It became a game in which I had to have the last word of a conversation. And, I was very quick and at ease doing so. But, there is more to the equation. My parents' generation were raised Catholic and, as such, there was much unpleasantness associated with my speaking out. I was punished more than a few times for being so vocal. I was supposed to learn to remain silent in many cases, because it's not right to speak out, or that you get punished when you verbalize your feelings.

Now, you have different examples of what my family dynamic was like. No wonder I became the voice of so many people, especially those who could hardly express their feelings! We all go through the wounds we receive in our youth, and my journey began with the choices I made in reaction to those wounds being inflicted. I came from a place of emotional sensitivity and I wonder if my outspokenness has something to do, at some level, with my difficulty saying no to people. I wonder, not to blame myself, but more out of a curiosity.

> *"Children are educated by what the grown-up is
> and not by his talk."*
> *– Carl Jung*

Starting My Journey

> *"Human faults are like garden weeds. They grow without cultivation and
> soon take over the place if they aren't thinned out."*
> *– Napoleon Hill*

So, now you better understand why I started out to find coaches, teachers, and people who could show me how to nurture and mentor the better parts of me so I could become successful in all the areas of my life. It was 2007 when I crossed the path of T. Harv Eker, the author of *Secrets of the Millionaire Mind*. During the seminar, "Millionaire Mind Intensive," I found my mind opening to a new model of success. As I applied his philosophy to my personality, thoughts, and actions, I began to have some significant insights.

First came the understanding that I had probably been sabotaging my success over the course of my 20-year career as an actress. One cause of that was my reaction to my parents' long-term lack of support for my work. Another was related to the fact that there were other people who, rather than giving me a hand up, were actually slowing me down. But, mostly, it was just me, and those twin devils called a lack of confidence and poor self-esteem. You see, people used to come up to me after headlining performances in plays and sing my praises, but I couldn't handle it; my power, my inner truth, and my light had all been diminished. I didn't feel I deserved their accolades.

I recognized that in the past I had not served myself in lots of ways. I took drugs to ease emotional pain and push down old feelings, had bad relationships and suffered from a generalized lack of self-respect. My life was such that I was giving myself away, piece by piece. Behind all of these destructive behaviours was the sexual abuse and harassment I mentioned earlier. Again, that abusive relationship has coloured all my other relation-ships. It's also incredibly sad, in fact disastrous, that I once helped out a friend of mine by giving his friend a ride back from a party, only to be raped in my own home as a result. The man to whom I was giving the lift had asked, while we were on the road, if he could come home with me and sleep on my living room couch. Perhaps I was naïve, but he was a friend of my friend, and so I had said yes. The rape temporarily crushed my spirit. It took a long time, and a lot of life experience, before I realized that nothing could break me, nothing or no one could keep me down, and that I was a force of nature.

I came to see that I wasn't a victim. I remembered that I had said "no" over and over and over, even to the point of screaming an endless scream. It was as if I came into a new world, ready to inspire myself with my courage, to stand up and speak my truth with compassion. I knew then that I would never be silenced or beaten down again.

Where I Was

"If you don't know why you failed, you are no wiser than when you began."
– Napoleon Hill

As I said above, I have been an actress for more than 20 years. Before these insights, I did not want to begin something else, even though I didn't really know how to handle the rollercoaster highs and lows that come along with being a busy, working actor who puts her whole life into each character for just $8,000 to $10,000 per year. Don't get me wrong; I was expecting a lot—fame, fortune, and going to New York to work. But, it seemed I was always in a place where I had to defend myself as an artist. I was doing well and had lots of work, but was living in poverty. Being poor takes all your energy, despite the fact that I was very good at being economical. I loved the work, but wasn't confident enough to make it through all the auditions. And, I wanted success, but I wasn't ready for it. I created a philosophy and mindset around being successful and not being able to handle it.

In short, I am a force of nature who was rebelling and taking drugs not to suffer. I was spending my energy on the wrong things and I became depressed at some level. I was wearing glasses through which I could not see. But, I fought my situation. Don't feel sorry for me, because there is nothing to be sorry about. I am a strong, courageous woman today, and these experiences are now just a part of my story. I just want you to feel respect for the woman I ended up being.

Where I Am Now

"Great achievement is born of a struggle."
– Napoleon Hill

I decided to be a businesswoman and to succeed no matter what. Many people take it for granted that being an entrepreneurial woman was easier for me because I am an actress. Not a chance! Too many years of being poor haunted my mind. And, I had to learn to stop arguing my point all the time, and listen to people. This was, and is, not always an easy thing to do. I'm still, sometimes, misinterpreted by others. Have you ever heard the expression, "What you see is what you get"? Well, I am who I am in the sense that what comes from my mouth is very direct and very much from the heart. The difference now is that I work on knowing when to "tell it like it is" and when to let the situation pass without comment.

Plus, I had a great fear of being successful — I was afraid of the emotional cost. Now, I have accepted the rules of the universe; I have learned to let the useless or counterproductive stories go. I understand that I have come to this earth to learn. All I have to do to make success happen is put myself out there, and the universe comes to me with its wisdom. I am strong, I am funny and I am devoted to helping others.

Of course, it took a bit of time for me to become that light that people can now see. And I deserve to show it. When some people say I am too much, I have choices. I can choose to respond rather than react, laugh instead of cry, speak up instead of being struck down, say "Stop lying to yourself"—whatever is needed.

So many of you who read this book will be surprised by my story as you have already (and only) experienced the joyful woman I have become, the one who has such a power of love and who is passionate, full of laughter and excited about relating to others and about giving them a hand. But, as you have started to see, the truth is that, not so long ago, my life was filled with such struggles and my blueprint had become that of a survivor. I fought against all odds to understand why I created and used an unhealthy pattern for such a long period of time.

Wherever you are in your life, I want you to know there is hope. There is always a way — even if you have screwed up like I have. I learned a lot when I chose the right to be once again respected as a woman. I reconstructed my self-esteem, my confidence and my relationships. Life sent me the lessons I learned in the form of aggression, and I am a success because I did not let that aggression keep me walled in.

I now embrace every challenge of my life because I am a force of nature. I have built everything on my own. And, I have conquered myself! I am so proud of this. Even though there was fire at my back, I rode the horse of my emotions until we were both free, and now that horse is magnificent. I wish the same type of transformation for you!

So, Why Write a Book?

"You have a book inside you and it's way passed time to get it out!"
– Raymond Aaron

I have repeated over and over to those who wanted to hear it, *"One day I will write my book!"* Then, like so many other people who say the same thing, I kept my writing at the bottom of a drawer. Each time I made a great discovery about my wounds or had a moment in which I was enlightened by some words of wisdom I heard, I would put pen to paper. But, then, my ego would get in the way and I would close the notebook.

The momentum to write kept coming back, but for far too long I suffered from impostor syndrome. I read so many beautiful, inspired writings and was guided by so many world-renowned authors that I told myself I wasn't good enough to write my book. But, then, inspiration knocked again. In 2008, I participated in the "Enlightened Warrior Training Camp," with Peak Potential. During this event, I felt the visceral urge to fill what I considered an essential missing part of my life path. When we were asked," If you were about to die today, what would you regret not having done in your life?" or "What do you crave doing before you die that will give you the satisfaction of having lived your life to the fullest?" sobs caught in my throat and I heard myself saying "My Book."

I could not leave this world without leaving a legacy of my quest for freedom and more meaning as a human being. Even though my journey is an intensive one, I needed to relive it. I had to give back and teach what I have overcome, and how I did it in the name of humanity. My insecure ego, of course, resurfaced, screaming, *"Who's interested?!"* I answered myself; this is the time to take control of my life, and writing my book is essential if I want to free myself from my own chains.

I crossed the path of Raymond Aaron in the fall of 2015. He was giving a presentation called "How to Write a Book" and inspired me right away. I literally began to shake inside. I couldn't ignore it any more. His passion was contagious. I can still hear Raymond saying, *"If you want to differentiate yourself from the rivers of the sea..."* The impulse I felt deep in my core was overwhelming, and I knew the time had come. He was the person who would help me realize my dream of being published. I had to honour my gift of putting emotions into words, use my verve and love of writing for my greatest happiness, and believe that people would have the desire to read what I wrote.

I have been inspired by others and know that it is now my time to inspire. Without pretense, I can say that it is my time to pay it forward. It is our duty to be the best human being we can be. You too have the right and ability to achieve similar success in your life. I'd like to ignite your inner strength and inspire you as I share my experience, knowledge, and courage with the world to help you unleash your personal essence and break through the wall that keeps you hemmed in. Please learn from your lessons and expand to manifest your personal essence.

I hope that I can inspire you, dear reader, and I would like to believe that you too can dare to discover the legacy of your passage on this earth. Whatever your ambitions are, everything is possible, and it is that message I wish to convey through the narrative of my humble story.

Chapter 2

My Quest for Freedom

"Freedom is not worth having it if it does not include the freedom to make mistakes."
— **Mahatma Gandhi**

For me, freedom means being able to live my own experiences fully, without the interference of anybody, based on their personal criteria. In my opinion, this is also a way to explore my horizons without being told what to do and how to do it. It is a way for me to play within my own boundaries and allow myself, if I choose, to expand my mind at my own pace. Of course, I am able to respectfully play by the rules of others, or a system, when this becomes necessary, as long it is my choice to do so. We always have the choice to use our discernment and withdraw from anything that no longer respects our deep values.

It can be very challenging to jump into the unknown and explore a new lifestyle but, after a while, you become more and more at ease with being in the state of mind to do so. And, it brings you all kind of support you wouldn't have necessarily expected, as you begin to spend more time with similarly-minded people. This is true whether we are talking about work or our social life. It's a matter of aligning yourself with others who choose to live spiritually and in alignment with the universe.

Now, as I've said, I'm a fighter. You will never see me quit. Of course, I have fallen, of course, I have failed, but I am able to handle myself. If I had given myself a chance to give up, I wouldn't be here. But, I have never given myself that choice. I'm an old soul, and maybe I didn't understand my wisdom and, perhaps, I didn't always understand my power, but everything I do comes from the heart. The fighter in me and the passion with which I approach life have always come through in such a way as to keep me moving forward rather than backward.

And so, when the time came, I was ready to receive the message of T. Harv Eker. After that seminar, I continued learning, especially from the wisdom of Napoleon Hill. Applying Hill's messages to my life helped me understand that I did not have to live in poverty. I began looking at my whole life and the choices I had been making. And, then I decided to make a brand-new choice.

My choice was, and is, to live a life of freedom — freedom from my past, freedom from my fears, freedom from financial insecurity, freedom from self-sabotage, and freedom from the opinions of others.

I hope that, after reading this book, you either pursue or continue your own quest for freedom. Mine is definitely what defines me best. Since I was young, I have always felt the need to explore and to not be limited by restrictions. So, what do you think life brought me? Of course, a family where rules were extremely important. And, oh, there were so many rules to follow. I didn't appreciate them at the time, but those rules helped me to be the person I am today. At the same time, they also caused me to be uncomfortable as I would not submit myself to them, just to prove I wasn't in agreement (talk about having to be right no matter what the cost).

First, Love Yourself

"You owe yourself the love that you so freely give to other people."
– Alexandra Elle

Freedom starts with believing in, loving and accepting yourself just the way you are. This is so much easier said than done. (We know it, right?) Not accepting myself for who I am was extraordinarily costly, especially in my relationships. I gave others permission to tell me who I was – or rather, who I should be. Instead of being real, I adjusted my behaviours to be the person they wanted, but underneath I was very resentful and my indignation would surface. At one point, this mindset caused a complete break with my parents; one with my father, and then one with my mother, as well; these breaks lasted for a full year or more.

There were also a lot of fights with my brother, who is very different from me. I'm fast, he's slow. We are both detail-oriented, but in different ways and, as such, I didn't have much patience with him. Neither of us was aware of how to support the other. I wasn't respectful to him because I could not see things from his point of view for such a long time. We make things in completely opposite ways and I had become very self-oriented, thinking I was the one who was right and good; he was wrong. It was sad because we deserved better from each other. Now I know that it's more about acknowledging our differences when we communicate with each other, and my relationship with him is much more fulfilling than it once was.

I want to tell you how I discovered that I was still lacking self-love and how I finally freed myself of the fear of being loved – even after years of working on myself.

Last year, I decided to follow a new program called "The Meaning Institute" with Marcia Wieder, the Founder of the program and CEO of Dream University®. I had already felt a connection with her at the heart and soul level and, because of that, had chosen her as my new spiritual teacher.

Marcia conducted our master class through a year-long program that was broken out into four modules. When the first module began in August of 2016, I knew there was something I had to reclaim, but I had no idea what it was. To say it another way, I was back, yet again, in the midst of another personal challenge. It was the kind of challenge in which you only see the "tip of the iceberg" (more on that later), and that obligates you to take a few steps back and evaluate another layer of what life has to teach you. Marcia calls life "The mystery school" as it always has something to teach us – whether that is to help us navigate through life with new practices and meaning, to open ourselves to the LOVE, to learn to nurture our heart, to discover the real meaning of the qualities of the heart, or to embody and accept ourselves. She helped us go through the process of reclaiming the lost parts of ourselves so we could become whole again.

Going forward, as we came to the process of the "Heart Initiation" ritual, I found myself literally shaking on the floor, just like a piece of bacon jumping in the pan while it cooks, because of the huge energy I began to feel inside of me. This may seem like an awkward sensation, but that's what happened as I began to open up slowly. It was as if my body's shell cracked and I became more and more able to receive the love being given by the other participants during my ritual initiation. I finally began to feel very good, and sense that the love was NOT going to hurt. I had to experience it at its core just so I could allow others to give me love and know that I was okay, and that nothing could happen to me as a grown woman who deserved and needed to be loved.

I was not expecting to have this reaction at all. I had been under the impression that I did love myself. After all, I am "a giver" who is aware of her weaknesses and has corrected so many of them to the best of her ability. I thought, *I am only human, right?* I had also taken on so many new good habits, such as choosing to eat healthy food and make time for myself, and I had been going to and studying at seminars for quite a few years. So, my impression was that in the doing all of those things, I was loving myself but, NO. I didn't!

Giving love seems easier to me than receiving it, just as I am sure it is for most of us. When I allowed myself to be loved and really felt it, I was moved to tears on a completely different and deeper level. It was incredible to feel the love others had for me, and to manifest it for others, as I recovered from having pushed love away for such a long period of time (during which I didn't know what it was to embody love). Have you observed how, sometimes, we give so much more love to others than we give to ourselves?

Self-criticism is so deeply anchored in us that it's part of our old habits. But, judging ourselves so harshly leads to bad consequences and plays against us. It biases our relationship with who we truly are. Sometimes, the way we treat ourselves on an unconscious level indicates a total lack of self-love. The Heart Initiation experience to embody love was just the beginning of my first real recovery. I could begin to allow my scars to heal by giving myself the love that I had expected others to provide (because I was unable to receive it from myself). Further, I saw that my self-destructive behaviors were consequences of the different types of abuse I had allowed to continue, thinking that, at least, my abusers were giving me some attention.

Accept Others For Who They Are

"Everything that irritates us about others can lead us to an understanding of ourselves."
– Carl Jung

When we accept ourselves, we can become more accepting of others as they are. It's liberating when you do this because you can then decide whether to keep that person in your life or let go of them for your own good. For example, I thought I could change my husband to fit the picture of what I wanted him to be. Does that sound familiar? Lots of women, maybe men as well (I don't know if it's more of a feminine trait) do the same thing as I did and have found that it is bound to lead to failure – and heartache – for both people. It's not healthy to tie ourselves to the wrong person, especially as it might keep us from finding the right one.

The same holds true in business. I have come to understand that I get a choice; I can decide who I want to work with. As an actress, I was so hungry to work that I would take every role that came along, even if I didn't feel right for the character, or the project wasn't a beautiful production. I didn't know that, by choosing whatever – a part or a business partner – I was sending the universe a message that is aligned with who I am (just as I didn't know how to choose a compatible man). I always doubted myself and my choices.

Now, I won't hang on or continue to work with a person for very long if they don't have the same values as I do. For example, I have and continue to work hard on improving myself so, if you are not fully motivated to getting better at whatever you want to be better at, I won't choose you for my team or partner with you. And, now, when I am confident that I am right about something, and the other person is not custom made for me, I would rather walk away from a project or someone than negotiate or try to bully them into changing their mind.

Behind-the-Scenes

*"Your willingness to look at your darkness is
what empowers you to change."*
– Iyanla Vanzant

As you read through this book, you will see many references to the fact that most of your challenges will take place "behind-the-scenes." In this context, it doesn't relate to acting, although you might have thought so because I'm an actress. For me, behind-the-scenes refers to the things we work on to change our thinking and behaviour.

For example, you may think that it would be natural and easy for me to be a leader because I'm an actress who can be funny and easily communicate with people. I heard that so often! But, it was far from easy. It's something I achieved. It is the work I've done searching within and outside of myself to access the power, fearless honesty, and genuine warmth I have for people that now allows me to lead teams. The intense study I've made of Napoleon Hill's principles, putting them into practice on a daily basis with my partners, and constantly correcting something or some behaviour as soon as I become aware of it, also have a great deal to do with my acquiring leadership skills. And, I have made tremendous efforts to grow when having courageous conversations in which I give feedback to people who were not listening to their associates or clients, but rather taking too much time trying to convince those other people that they were right. Since I, too, had gone through the same thing, I could show them how to change while someone else could not. One should know which new abilities have to be developed to become a better coach or teacher, as well as are what will make you a greater leader. This may apply in every area of our lives. Skills are skills!

Today, people instinctively choose to follow me because of what I embody. And that beingness comes from all the hard work I've done as part of my release process. I have learned how to be much more emotionally detached instead of having quick reactions that don't serve me well. It took a lot of practice and compassion for myself when cleaning up my bad habits. Relating to people can be very challenging and I used to say things without filtering them, which roiled up the fire when I was not necessarily intending to do so. At least I could stay aware of how I was acting and apologize when needed.

Not everything that goes on behind-the-scenes is positive or constructive. For example, my grandmother used to tell me *"Don't laugh so loud; it's not appropriate for a girl."* Or she would often say, *"Stop laughing that way."* I allowed these slights to affect me deeply. With my parents, what I heard a lot was *"You can't do this, you can't say that"* or *"No, not this way."* Even if I had done 90% of something the right way, I focused on the 10% that was negative or not perfect.

As a result of these criticisms or attacks on my personality, I became a chameleon. I felt I had to be the "right" person for each and every one with whom I came into contact. I even thought I had to ask permission from others just to speak, and used to always raise my hand in meetings. I would then get irritated by people who jumped into a conversation without having asked permission. So, my way of doing things was conditioned by whether or not it was okay to do it. And now I know that I am repeating the pattern when I hear myself apologize by habit. Today, I know that this is irrelevant. And, I let people talk when that happens but, inside of me, I shouldn't allow other people's crap to bother me. I deserve more, and so do you!

Expectations

"Find the courage to ask questions and express what you really want."
– **Don Miguel Ruiz**

We all have expectations, whether that means believing that something will happen (like closing a sale or getting a bonus) or that someone will think or act a certain way. Trouble comes when our expectations aren't met, perhaps because we wanted too much from someone or misread a situation. No matter what creates our expectations they must be looked at carefully, especially when building a team, dealing with employees in your company, leading a training session or even when creating harmonious relationships with friends, family or your mate.

I learned why we create expectations when Guylaine Grenier talked about the necessity of knowing our own needs and going beyond our initial temptation to take for granted that someone will exhibit a certain behaviour that meets those needs. Making such an assumption leads us to judge that person or group of people badly. The greatest disappointments and arguments come when we expect something and don't get it. It's critical to know whether the person you expect to do something is not capable of doing it, or if what you want is unrealistic. Instead, we should validate our perceptions beforehand. Guylaine is a psychosociologist and an accredited trainer and coach. In this particular context, she was training trainers. She created a "Reality Training" so people could learn and practice a methodology for handling other people in difficult situations when they occur.

I was hired as an actress to be a tool the participants used to turn theory into practice. We did a lot of work together, as Guylaine held the training for quite a few companies at the time. At one point in the training, Guylaine taught the participants how important it is to discover the fundamental needs of a human being. Let's take a quick look at them: to be seen, to be listened to, to be protected, to succeed and to be respected in our identity. I name them here because people tend to ignore how important they are to everything in our lives. They are the criteria against which we judge whether our needs are being fulfilled or not.

Our expectations and the degree to which they can be met determines whether two people can collaborate well. The clue to establishing and continuing a better collaboration is to ask good questions in the first place. We must recognize and claim what can be called the hidden parts of what we project, as these sometimes lead to miscommunication.

Although the "Reality Training" was initially a job, it really became a school for me as well, because of all the preparation we had to do before we met the clients each time. You see, as I was roleplaying in Guylaine's program, the participants were allowed, when needed, to ask what I was thinking, that is, what the character in the game was thinking. I came to understand what creates unharmonious communications in my own life. It became obvious to me when I was explaining to the participants why I wasn't in a collaborative mood (for instance, because they were challenging me as the character), and Guylaine was helping them express their needs by using the communication tools she was teaching them about. The participants' goal was to keep practicing through our real-life conversations until they realized which tool to use to go beyond the obvious and create a mutually better point of understanding. It was also very enlightening for me to keep repeating the behaviours that pushed people's buttons until they learned how to express their needs.

Usually, everyone has good intentions initially, but things get complicated because we protect ourselves, hiding the needs we have that haven't been taken care of. We don't know how to express them, and that's where the problem starts. In a lot of cases, when your intention is clearly to reclaim peace, it's most appropriate to be brave and become vulnerable, to open your heart and talk about which of the other person's behaviours have harmed you. Using the facts as starting points, express how you were affected. Doing it this way brings the other person more in alignment with their responsibility rather than pushing them into defense mode, which is counterproductive in that both of you will likely continue to dig your heels in. Ask the other person if there is something that can be done to help, and what agreement can be reached. If the conversation is about a recurring situation, encourage the other person to express their own insights, and find a solution together.

Sometimes, we have to disengage ourselves from people who just are not respecting us. But, keep in mind that it is better when we fulfill our expectations ourselves, and you get a better result when you tell them what you need.

Today, I have a better understanding of why people are resistant to expressing what they need and why so much of the other person's behaviour (or ours) seems inappropriate or in direct opposition of how we expect them to behave. It happens when we keep silent instead of sharing our thoughts with each other. We are better off finding the courage we need to validate *our* perceptions and ask if something happened which led to the behaviour that hurt or upset us. Better still is coming to an agreement before trouble starts. There are some rules we can apply in such situations, especially in setting agreements and establishing responsibilities, that prove extremely helpful.

It took me quite a while to understand how to create an agreement, correctly establish rules with my partners and associates, and talk about what to do *if our* agreements are in any way lacking integrity. In the past, I was afraid of appearing rigid or stiff but, in truth, the exact opposite became true. My old agreements didn't always include the right to have one's time and space respected. As such, I was respectful of others' boundaries, but never put up my own. This caused me to doubt myself a lot, and to wonder what was going on in my head that led to so many awkward responses. From this, I became aware of my own patterns, letting others take responsibility for what was to be done and when or where it would happen. (Sound familiar? ha, ha, ha) I finally got to the point where I could be sensible instead of silent. And, I found that handling and managing the people who disempower us is sometimes the best way to gain their respect. (This is easier said than done.)

Usually, people are unaware that their actions and words are upsetting to us or go against our values. There have been times when I did a poor job of managing my own expectations and hoped that my lover, my parents or a colleague would figure out – all on their own – what my needs were, and then fulfill them. When these people didn't "read my mind," I would initially keep my mouth shut until I exploded in anger because they didn't know what I needed without being told.

Know how to create a level of collaboration when people give you a hard time. Understand what caused the misunderstandings. When we look closer at a situation, we find we are always part of it.

You Deserve the Best!

*"Always know the difference between
what you're getting and what you deserve."*
– Unknown

In the past, I tried to convince myself that I was comfortable with what I had. But it was only when my quality of life had been really improved that I could see the difference. And, I do not even speak here about luxury, but of a quality of life that allows me to be free to travel outside of a regular agenda, and to do what I like, without having to refuse an invitation because I am economically limited and living on a budget. Realizing my first dream, living in my own home, has been an inexhaustible source of happiness for me. It has certainly contributed to my feeling proud of myself for having put in the necessary effort to achieve this goal. As an actress, I was confined to staying in a three-and-a-half-room apartment pretending that I was happy, but I was not.

For me, the phrase "You deserve the best" also means not buying my clothes in a second-hand shop any more, being able to get a massage, enjoying a spontaneous show with friends, buying myself some flowers, and decorating my yards. Whether it is products to buy, a business opportunity you are able to invest in, or something in your personal life you want, you are entitled to offer it to yourself. We don't need anyone else's permission to be successful and enjoy the best, but we may need to give ourselves permission to succeed. I had to refurbish my self-worth before I could accept this fact. And, now that I have made a major shift in my quality of life, I know the real meaning of "why I deserve the best" in all areas of my life. More than that, I set the criteria for what is best, and it is a reflection of me and my desires.

So, yes, success is a choice; one you make each minute of every day by taking action to achieve it. You must decide. Do you choose to move forward or do you choose to move backward? Do you know that standing still is the same or worse than moving backward? Do you laugh or do you cry? Do you say yes to what lies before you or do you say no? Will you do the right thing or the wrong thing? Will you choose to move through life by being present at all times or will you be like the masses and sleepwalk through the days of your life?

I hope this book shakes you up a little bit and really helps you make the right choices, because you deserve the best. Why can I say that? Because I used to sleepwalk before my awakening and I've walked the walk. I now know that we all deserve the best. When I learned to receive and began to enjoy the path of the journey I was on, I realized that I deserved the good that was happening. These things were coming through me, were being made by my choices, and I deserved the harvest of my planting.

Be Your Own Best Friend

"There comes a point when you have to realize that you'll never be good enough for some people."
– Unknown

You have to be your own best friend, and that requires valuing yourself above others. I am not talking about being selfish. We must treat ourselves as we would treat someone dear to us. I learned this the hard way when a group of people chose to leave me out of something we used to do together, even though I had given many of them a hand in the past. They had their reasons for ignoring me, but it doesn't matter what those reasons were or whether they were valid; that's not the point of telling you about what happened.

What matters is how I perceived their actions. In reality, it was their problem, but it became mine as long as I gave it my attention. I thought that it was about me, and this is how we poison ourselves, by taking things personally. We have to become mindful of our projections and the way we presume. And, this is exactly what I perceived: I felt rejected, so I presumed that I was the one who was in trouble or had the problem. Even if something mean or bad is done to us purposely, it is crucial to be able to detach ourselves from the people involved or the situation and to give ourselves the same type of support we would naturally give a friend. To do this, I had to develop a new relationship with myself.

Just as when we are first getting to know someone else, I had to learn about who I really was and start trusting myself more deeply to keep my bliss and stop giving myself away to people who didn't support me. I am not my best friend when I consider others to be better or more deserving than I am. I had to ask myself, "Why do I wish for others to receive the blessings of the world, but not me?" I suffered a lot when I was rejected by people I love, people who I had served over the last couple of years. But, I must remember that some people will stay in our life for only a day, some will remain for just a season and some others will stay and live side-by side with us for our whole life.

I saw myself as a victim for far too long and, on an unconscious level, gave everything to others so they would like me. I thought I was serving people who respected me and I expected that my efforts would come back to me in another form. Why was I always the last one to benefit from my time and effort?

This was true in all parts of my life, not just in business, but also with my husband and my ex-boyfriends; it was always the same. I was someone who seemed to be waiting for others in order to live, or at least to be happy. Guess what I discovered about all this when I unveiled another layer of comprehension? When you don't show up for yourself, the universe sends you certain types of people who will give you the opportunity to look in the mirror and see how you treat yourself. Wow! Let me say to you, I started to show up for myself.

Here's another example: I was always doing the things I loved in a rush instead of taking the time to enjoy the experience; I deprived myself in order to run off and help someone else. And, I was always crossing the boundaries I put around what I deserved, which was to rest or to play. I had to take myself out of my own way. I had to find my place where respect and deservedness were allowed, and where I was not trying to compare myself to or please others. I had to be somewhere I didn't have to fight for my place, and I could take some time to embody my strength and get my power back so I could become centred and aligned with my own heart.

Remember to always pay yourself first.

Have Forgiveness

*"Our ability to handle life's challenges is
a measure of our strength of character."*
– Les Brown

Forgiving myself and others is a supremely powerful action, and it has given me the peace that allows my spirit to be free. Everyone needs to accept their life path and learn. When I am truly wronged, even though it's difficult to do so, I can forgive. And, that forgiving gives me peace of mind. The process of learning how to really forgive myself began when I was called to audition for a commercial "against aggression." We actors were asked to speak in front of the camera as if we were talking directly to our aggressor in a private home video. So, I presented myself as I usually do, and asked this question before we started: *"Do you know that one out of three women is a victim of aggression?"* There was a huge silence on the set, and then a woman's voice respectfully said, "Yes!"

I continued nervously, *"Because your script is my story."* I just stated it as a fact. I said, *"I wonder, how do you see the character? Because, I can play it whatever way depending on the needs."* She said, *"We see her not as a victim anymore, but still want to show her emotional scars."* So, I added, *"I personally faced my abuser, two months ago, and I know the feeling – how it feels – but I haven't had the chance to say what I am about to perform."* The woman who had answered me before said, *"I would be interested in your version. Please just talk to him directly."*

From that very moment, I knew – EXACTLY – that I was meant to be a voice for the victims, one of the spokespersons for this powerful message. It was a bridge to helping victims of aggression denounce their aggressors. My friend Guylaine's brother is a cop and he told me later that my commercial had kept the police as busy as ever for a really long period of time, because they were receiving calls daily as victims massively stepped into the denunciation process.

But, my healing was just about to begin. When I saw the commercial for the first time, and every time thereafter for a year and a half (it became a primetime commercial, running everywhere), I ran to the shower and cried. My wounds totally reopened; it felt like my legs were too heavy to support me and I stayed in the bath, losing track of time for at least an hour.

During this period of time, it felt like I was sleepwalking because people recognized me in the street everywhere I went. They would share personal confidences or show in their eyes that they were uncertain about what to do – should they congratulate me for my acting or did it really happen to me? Some dared to ask me the question directly, and I began to say, *"Yes, it is my story as well."* A friend even called me one day to say, *"Turn on your TV."* They were repeating my commercial during a one-hour special in which we could hear victims' testimonials of how they went through their process. Some said to call the police and to follow the steps, while others explained their fear of doing it. I listened for a bit but decided to shut down the TV because it reminded me that I was one of them, and that I hadn't named either my abuser or my aggressor.

A few months after the commercial was on, I was invited to a celebration gathering at the summer theatre where I had acted. We toasted our success and shared all the photos and frames of all the plays we had performed in during all of our years together. This celebration occurred on my 44th birthday. Originally, I was not sure if I should go, but then decided that I would be denying myself too much if I gave in to the fear of seeing my abuser again.

On the way there, as I was about to cross the last curve of the highway and reach the exit, I could feel my heartbeat. I looked at all the cars in the theatre's parking lot and began to feel nervous. I didn't feel good at all and I sat in my parked car for a minute or two. Then, it hit me! I had absolutely nothing to be ashamed of! I looked at myself in the mirror, took a deep breath trying to forgive him when, much to my surprise, I received this answer from deep within me: *I need to forgive myself!* I was the one who had given my power to this man, and I hated him for it. But, if I was to show my shame and fear at the celebration, he would win again. As soon as I realized this, I felt the release of my shame and the power of forgiveness for myself. I began to smile and thought, *Wow, he is the one who needs the help.* I had mercy for him and my emotions left me like the whoosh of an emptying balloon. I pulled myself together and went to meet all of my other friends.

I looked at him during that afternoon to see if he was trying to look at me in any way and, not only did he not try to talk to me, he even left the party early –something he would never have done before. He had been the only person not to congratulate me on the commercial; everyone else came to me to let me know how powerful it was and how good I was, "as always!" The whole situation made me feel terribly uncomfortable, especially as only two or three close friends knew what had happened with him. But, this time I thanked everyone for their kind words. I have to say, this birthday represented a rebirth, and the beginning of my healing journey. And, all this happened in the very same place where everything had started 26 years ago.

You see, when I was pointing at my abuser for making my life a "whole shit," I could see nothing else. But, as soon as I forgave myself, he was forgiven as well, and I realized he was one of my biggest teachers in life. Before I forgave, I felt anger. I felt trapped, violated, and stuck as if I was in prison. Forgiving him helped me tremendously as it was the first time I understood the concept and power of forgiveness.

Forgiveness is the capacity to overcome anger and let the hurting go. It's when you no longer identify yourself as the target. The sickness comes from the abuser. Forgiveness is also an act of compassion toward ourselves, someone else or something that happened for which we need to give ourselves some love. It is always better to begin with forgiving ourselves. I have made forgiving part of the pattern of my behaviour, and I always start with myself.

Here is another example of what I'm talking about: I had "an adventure" when I was 26 years old, the result of which was that I became pregnant. I knew from the very beginning that I had to deal with this alone, and decided to go into a women's centre, to give myself space and time to be at one with my decision. I wrote a letter to my unborn child explaining why I could not welcome his beautiful soul into my world. I wrote about being a wounded child myself and how there was too much hurt in my life, as well as how I had been irresponsible by not using protection when I was with someone who was almost a stranger to me.

It took me a while, and the learning of a few rules of the road, to grasp the wisdom in also forgiving myself for two other unborn children; I kept blaming myself for repeating my mistakes, but becoming ready to forgive myself helped me forgive the people I most needed to forgive. Realizing that a lot of my unhappiness came from the patterns I had put into place forced me to understand the real meaning of forgiveness.

It is my awareness, resilience, commitment, and willpower that allows me to forgive.

I attended a once in a lifetime seminar in 2009 called "All Your Relations" with T. Harv Eker, Marianne Williamson, and a few other renowned speakers. At some point, they were talking about how we embody real forgiveness toward those to whom we are related. We had to do an exercise, to write a letter to someone we struggle with and lay out all the wrongs done by that person ("You have made this or that which caused this to me...you hurt me when you said this to me... you, you, you"). We were then to circle the word "you" every time it appeared and change it to "I."

I'd like to ask you to put this book down for a moment and try the exercise yourself. Spend some time and write your own letter to someone who, to this day, is really hurting you. Write everything that comes to your mind. Then circle all the "yous" and substitute the word "I." Please continue reading right after doing this exercise.

Oh, my God! It's huge, right? We must be able to let go of the emotions and resentments that trap us into giving away our power, and that comes from forgiving ourselves. For the seminar, I wrote my letter to my father and discovered, after reading it, that I had a lot of things in common with him, for which I was blaming him. This breakthrough allowed me to heal some part of my own shadow. Once we completed the exercise and had shared about it, I walked away feeling much less weighted down. I became more aware of who I really was. At that seminar, I thought that I had forgiven my abuser but, as you just read, there was a deeper layer of anger and resentment to un-root.

I hope you can feel the power of this healing, and I hope that you can relate to it as well. It's important to come to understand the importance of stopping the urge to blame others in total for something they have done to hurt you. In truth, we all contribute to these events, we all have a part in it and we have to look at ourselves at some level.

Look at whatever it is closely and see how transformative this action can be.

What's Holding You Back?

"The moment you commit and quit holding back, all sorts of unforeseen incidents, meetings and material assistance will rise up to help you."
– Napoleon Hill

It's a simple question, and I have asked it of myself many times. The answer doesn't need to be complicated. For example, even though I was a fighter pushing myself, I was unable to see myself living in success. This failure to visualize, to actually see the thing I wanted clearly in my mind, was part of what was holding me back. Being resentful and feeling unworthy also deterred me from achieving the things I wanted.

Learning how to "respect thyself" is one of the most powerful healings I have ever had. Now, my journey has brought me to a place where I can show people there is hope somewhere, even though what they may be experiencing seems like the biggest injustice possible. Even though the universe continues to test me, to see if I have learned the lesson of self-respect, I am in a higher place than those who disrespect me. The things they say could poison me if I let them, but I don't. You can get there too.

What's holding you back? Are you holding on to resentments? Are those resentments still benefiting you in any way? What truly no longer serves you? Does it happen that you blame people from your past for what's wrong in your life today? Are old behaviours and feelings about yourself sabotaging today's victories?

Jump Into Your Greatness

*"You are being called to live a bigger life. Answer the call.
Playing small doesn't serve you."*
– Les Brown

The world is a mirror through which we can consciously adjust ourselves. Don't waste another day. See yourself in the mirror of the world and jump into your own greatness. Be honest about what you see in that mirror. Stop lying to yourself! I have made it half way through my journey to financial freedom and have realized it is priceless to do whatever it takes. Letting go was the answer, of course. I had lots of things to let go: my false beliefs, my willingness to be right, and my overdeveloped sense of pride. I have also had to let go of how people see me. Of course, it took courage to stand up and transform my life. But, at the age of 45, I loved life too much to be sitting in a living room watching TV and not having the lifestyle I deserved. So, look hard at your life through the mirror that is the world around you. And, if you don't like what you see, let go of the story that is keeping you there.

Becoming a Leader

*"Watch the one ahead of you, and you'll learn why he is ahead.
Then emulate him"*
– Napoleon Hill

It took me a few years into my process of becoming a true leader to understand what attracts and what repels based on my energetic businesslike manner. As a sensitive and passionate woman, and to the detriment of my own success, I often confused my natural instinct to be a driving force with my overambitious ways. I had to ask myself how I could better drive people to follow me using the right communication skills; that is, the ones that make people follow you because they choose you.

After I had made a lot of mistakes, I decided to study so I could master the communication strategies that I needed to learn. In July of 2016 I attended an "Ultimate Leadership Camp," which lasted five full days and nights. We were taught how to give and receive positive, constructive feedback in a context that compelled us to master and embody the skills we were learning. During these practices, we were led to make critical decisions under a huge amount of pressure so that we could truly live the new communication skills we were learning. Each day, I had another huge breakthrough and I stepped up to really master the practice sessions, which were held outside and on the ground. The sessions were very realistic in that there were hard consequences if we did not succeed, and we had to keep at it until we did.

I had already learned the value of being a strong leader before I attended this camp. It happened at a Training Retreat, a full-day mentoring session called "The Ultimate Training," and it was held before our big annual convention. I discovered that I had a natural sense of leadership, but that it needed to be polished and empowered. At the time, I was reading *The Soul of Leadership: Unlocking Your Potential for Greatness* by Deepak Chopra, which is a great piece of artistry, and also opened my consciousness about my natural talent and abilities.

Nothing can replace the kinaesthetic memory in our body, whether we learn it from our own mistakes in life or a transformational experience during training to discover how to behave as a leader. I came back from each of these two trainings with a lot of humility and a better awareness of what new principles I needed to master so I could bring both a better plan and better instructions to my team. This is where I became conscious of how, before that, I quite frequently and unconsciously disempowered others when trying to be their leader. My preference for being a loner didn't help the situation.

The camp also showed me how to become a strong second-in-command as well. This is crucial if you want to achieve your next level of success or accomplishment. Before you can lead others, you must lead yourself! Only then will you be able to empower others to lead as well, as you assist them in reaching their next level by continuing the powerful skill of delegation.

I could not possibly have accepted these leadership skills before I began my journey of learning and growth. After all, it is very hard to see yourself as — or be — a leader when you think of yourself as always being in the wrong. I was living on a lower vibration then. Now, knowing when I am right, I am able to address other people with dignity and compassion.

After "The Ultimate Training" I found an eloquent statement by a mentor of mine that was posted on Facebook; I kept it to remind me of who I AM. Here are his words:

"Have you ever felt misunderstood? Have you ever felt like you had no one to talk to who could understand?

Have you ever felt that you were the only one who could clearly see the vision?

Have you ever felt the pain of betrayal? Have you ever felt you were always the subject of gossip? Have you ever felt like you were being judged?

Have you ever felt like giving up but knew that you couldn't due to the promises you made?

Have you ever felt like people show you the side of them they want you to see in order to benefit from what you have to offer? But you allow them to act it out without challenging them because your goals are bigger than their insecurities?

Have you ever had moments where you said "I must be crazy to think this way?"

Have you ever felt alone but surrounded by so many people?

Have you ever felt that many of the freedoms you once enjoyed were replaced by responsibilities?

Have you ever felt the pressure of serving those who would plot against you?

Have you ever felt that no matter how much you give to others, it's never enough?

Have you ever felt like you live in a glass house? Have you ever asked yourself, "Why am I continuing to do this?"

If you have experienced most of these situations...Welcome to the World of Leadership!

The call of a Leader is not for the faint of heart or the ill prepared. Be mindful of who you label as a leader. A big check DOES NOT automatically equate to a leader. It sometimes means that you got in first or that you simply outworked everyone! It takes up to 18 months to develop a big check. But it takes 3-5 years to develop a leader. Low standards for leadership leads to instability in the pursuit of your mission! Stand Strong!"

– H.B.

Not only have I asked myself these questions, but I have also gone through each of them during heartbreaking experiences... and I have overcome them all! I am so honoured and grateful to be associated with an organization known for its high level of integrity, and learning from the mentors I follow, each of whom also has such a high level of integrity.

What would the answers be if you were to ask yourself the same questions? I hope that reading what this mentor has written will help you find the answers you seek without all of the pain I had to experience to get where I am – and where I will be as I continue my life's journey.

Chapter 3

Embrace the Challenge

"Every adversity, every unpleasant circumstance, every failure, and every physical pain carries with it the seed of an equivalent benefit."
– Napoleon Hill

Taking responsibility for your life and your actions is a challenge, but it is one that brings great rewards. I have embraced every challenge that life has sent me. Doing so has made changes for the better in my own life. The concept represents something that my parents, especially my father, tried to teach me, but I didn't really understand its full meaning at the time.

I had to learn to make myself accountable for my actions and not for the actions of others. What others do that affects me is their responsibility. The things I do as a response to what they have done — for that I am accountable. I have choices, and the choices I make have consequences. I embrace the challenge of making the right choices so that I can have positive consequences. I also dare to mention that each time I have to embrace adversity, I go to sleep at night knowing that, at least, I will always be able to look at myself in the mirror and see how much I have overcome the results that came from behaving stupidly. In truth, you'll notice, as we move ahead in this book, that I wholeheartedly embraced quite a few of those experiences or actions.

Transcend Old Wounds

"If it doesn't challenge you, it won't change you."
– Unknown

Taking responsibility for your own actions in life will empower you to grow a thicker skin, but blaming yourself for what someone else has done to you is quite another thing. If you are like a lot of victims, you probably blamed yourself for what happened even though you did nothing wrong. I have been a victim of injustice more than once and I know the pattern all too well. I used to nurse the wounds inflicted on me by others and repeatedly pointed my finger at the offender without understanding what I was actually doing.

To be able to embrace the challenge, I had to transcend my wounds and find the wisdom in what happened. I learned how to use my pain, heal myself, and accept others as they are without wasting my energy trying to change them or resenting them. Regardless of their actions or the feelings they project, most people are giving their best, one day at a time. So, it's critical to stop pointing at and blaming others. Instead, I now try to see past the behaviours I don't understand and peek at a person's behind-the-scenes. They may be dealing with some personal crisis or recent bad news. They may have had a terrible fight with their partner that morning or whatever. I know when to forgive, when to help, and when to walk away without diminishing my own power in the process.

And, now, I say it's a choice between reacting and acting; it's about learning to respond to a person or situation without letting my emotions take over. I also make the choice to say, yes, this happened to me, whatever it is that happened – but it does not control me anymore. It does not change who I am. And, most importantly, it does not serve me anymore. Today, I choose not to be a victim. Instead, I choose to be an enlightened warrior, something that comes from my true self. It's so important because, if I lose my power, I'm back in the victim mode. Don't let that happen to you.

This may or may not be the challenge you are facing, but the things I've learned from embracing my challenges are universal. The things we want most in life do not come without struggle and hard work. So, whatever challenge you face, embrace it as best you can. Take it on with a wiser attitude and focus on the wonderful outcome that lies on the other side of that challenge. The road to success is paved with hard work, self-searching, and the overcoming of our own behaviours and beliefs that hold us back. In many ways, the latter is the biggest and most universal challenge of all, and the battles we all face go on behind-the-scenes.

The going may be difficult, and it may often feel like there is just too much to handle, but we can handle it, and will have to do so sooner or later. The universe will make certain we do. How else can it teach us the lessons it keeps in its back pocket? We need to be flexible or the universe will bring us to the floor so we can loosen our resistance. My closest friends have witnessed me while I was in this process, and believe me, I know what I am talking about when I say the universe compels you to master new abilities. I haven't just been taught the skills I've learned on my journey once. No, there have been turning points that brought me to the floor yet again and I have lived at the deepest level of my being when I brought myself to point of burnout. My only choice was to kill off my old self and experience a rebirth to embody the new me.

Facing your challenges head on is so rewarding!

> *"Adversity will do something to you or of you..."*
> *– Napoleon Hill*

Accept Who You Are

> *"We cannot change anything until we accept it.*
> *Condemnation does not liberate, it oppresses."*
> *– Carl Jung*

I know that I have already touched on how self-destructive it is not to accept yourself but, as it has probably cost me the most in life, I need to share some more of my thoughts on the subject. As I've said, I gave others permission to tell me who I was, thinking that I had to adjust and be the person they saw instead of who I really am. Not only have I been hard on myself, I have been too hard on others, even those dealing with the same issues that I am.

I had to accept myself just as I was before I could try to refine my beliefs and behaviours with detachment. Reaching a point where I could be non-judgmental allowed me to decide which behaviours were useful and which ones were not getting me what I wanted. Plus, feeling bad about those parts of my personality was exhausting and unproductive, as was justifying why I was the way I was.

Do you know how to connect with the right people for you?

If you want to attract people into your life who are aligned with you and the way you work, you have to master some skills, especially a new way of speaking. I learned that I didn't have to change myself, but I did have to adjust the way I communicate in specific situations. I can be emotional and passionate, as can a lot of people. In business, that often works more appropriately with women, but less so with men.

Everyone also needs to accept that you are who you are and that is OK! It's not about judging us to be a bad person or a mean one. We are all human beings who can choose to change our actions — not because we are wrong — but because, maybe, we are not producing the positive results we want.

Accepting who you are is the result of being willing to grow so you can get the changes you want for yourself.

Do you have respect for yourself? Or do you beat yourself up all the time? Do you criticize yourself, regret the things you've said or done simply because someone else said it wasn't the right thing to do or say? Does inner turmoil cause you to self-sabotage, to screw up, and confuse things? If your answer to these questions is yes, then you too have a problem respecting yourself for who you are. Believe me; I understand as only one who has come from the same place can.

Embrace the Challenge

Conquer Thyself

"He who conquers others is strong; he who conquers himself is mighty."
– Lao Tzu, Chinese Philosopher

Another critical part of my story is one of injustice. Looking at my life from that perspective left me feeling defeated and insecure. To get on the path to success I had to let go of my negative attitudes; they were keeping me from reaching my full potential. I also realized that the results of my own reactions and behaviours left me aligned with defeat and lacking in self-confidence.

Living without self-respect was quite hard, and learning to respect myself is one of the truly powerful growth experiences I have ever had. I think it is something I had subconsciously chosen for myself so that I could learn how to help others find hope. I am now able to tell people going through what seems like the biggest injustice that there is hope somewhere.

What happened to change me? I realized I was allowing what other people thought — and what I thought they were thinking and saying — to keep me stuck in place, making assumptions and trying to defend myself, letting their toxic words and actions affect my self-confidence. In turn, that kept me from moving forward. In the end, I came to understand that those other people were really talking about themselves, not me. I learned that I can be at a higher level.

Be Passionate

"Enthusiasm changes lives… Excite the imagination of others; inspire their creative vision; help them connect with Infinite Intelligence."
– Napoleon Hill

Passion and enthusiasm help to propel us forward into greatness. Passion is what makes us take on and win any challenge and last through any adversity. It is not the same for everyone so, if you're not connected to something that drives you, then you must discover and define it first. Purpose brings passion.

During "The Ultimate Leadership Camp" that I attended last summer, we were taught, among other things, how to distinguish between passion and emotion, the definitions of which are vastly different. This distinction became really helpful to me, as I used to confuse the two. Passion is an inner sense of excitement that inspires people. It is contagious, positive, and attracts others. Passion comes from connecting your heart with your integrity and it leads you to take actions that are the personification of this inner driving force. Emotions, when they are not delivered accurately, may create huge secondary effects you did not intend to have happen.

I now understand what brought on my overwhelming volcano of emotions, as well as how it affected people and why it was not inspiring. I became aware that one of my natural gifts is to be inspiring as I am, by instinct, a passionate woman. In the past, when I didn't contain my emotional enthusiasm, I was more than capable of blowing people away, and not in a good way. I could act out of proportion to the situation, which was detrimental. This is one of my shadows of which I must be aware. And, I must acknowledge that my dysfunctions are my inner child, who needs my attention.

It hit me when someone said, *"When emotion is high, intelligence is low."* (ha, ha, ha, boy did I know what that meant.) Now, I embody the spirit of enthusiasm in heartfelt ways that connect people and I use my passion with discernment, which means I lead people from a very different standpoint. I found it so powerful to just reclaim this innate gift and let go of what can be called my unbridled enthusiasm. My passion is what keeps me going every day, but I had to learn to control my emotions if I wanted to succeed. I could not have gotten to where I am today without being passionate about the challenges in my life and about the seminars, training sessions, and coaching that have helped me obtain my freedom and my success. The universe sends me things because I have passion. As an artist, my passion is my fuel, and it's a great gift that allows me to be a magnet. Consider how you want to be a magnet for people.

Have Commitment

"Honor your commitments with integrity."
– Les Brown

My level of commitment is huge, and you will need to be just as dedicated to the things you engage in and the lessons you want to learn. From the teachings of Napoleon Hill's *Keys to Success*, I have come to expect certain things from my business partners. If they don't take the opportunity seriously from the beginning, then they don't deserve my time. I can't let their lack of focus or commitment slow me down. I am dedicated to achieving success and I won't work with people who can't help me get there anymore.

Today, I have new and more successful people in my life than there were in the past. Teamwork has helped my business reach the volume of a Starbucks' outlet. I've also achieved this level because of my determination and commitment. I visualized my success and worked even harder on my personality and my weaknesses. When I embrace a challenge or go after something, I leave the weak part of me behind, and use willpower and the highest level of manifestation to create and attract what I want.

Take Responsibility

"The difficulty we have in accepting responsibility for our behavior lies in the desire to avoid the pain of the consequences of that behavior."
– Scott Peck

Taking on any challenge must be done with integrity. It calls for being accountable, not just to others but, most of all, to yourself. It took quite a bit of behind-the-scenes work for me to come to this critical conclusion about being responsible, and to put it into place in my own life. Imagine my amazement at seeing that I am really good at it! First, I had to learn the true meaning of responsibility. I used to equate the word with something my parents, specifically my father (who often called me a dreamer), expected from me and from which I rebelled. But, being responsible is not about doing what others consider the responsible thing. It's about being responsible to yourself and for your actions.

Before my inner journey started, I most certainly didn't understand the importance of bringing this concept into my own life. I now know that I must make myself accountable, not just to or for others, but to myself first. If I take an action, it is a choice that I have made, and that obliges me to take responsibility for it, whether I am happy with the results of that action or not. I also now know that I get to decide if I want to do something or not; I can do it if I want to, and de-commit if I don't. Again, I am accountable for what comes from making the choices I make.

Think Before You Choose

"When you are immune to the opinion and the actions of others, you won't be the victim of needless suffering."
– Don Miguel Ruiz

The co-founder of the company I am associated with studied Napoleon Hill's principles at the age of 19 and achieved success at a very young age. He is world-renowned and has received countless rewards and accolades. This humble, successful mentor is a total inspiration to me, and was instrumental in teaching me a hugely helpful lesson when I was dealing with a betrayal, the details of which are not important at this point. He knew that I was upset and, despite his incredibly busy schedule, asked to see me. We had a full ten-minute meeting in which he talked about making wise choices rather than easy or immediate ones.

I came to the meeting with paper and pen, expecting to take great notes as he shared his wisdom with me. But, he threw me a bit off-guard when he started the meeting by asking me a question. He wanted me to assess how much negativity I had in my life. He told me to include everything to which I could add the word "negative" as an adjective. I didn't quite know how to answer him, although there were a lot of negative things going on in my life. When he could see I was a bit hesitant, he took my notebook and pen and said in a warm and humorous tone, *"As I see, you take good notes. Here's what I want you to*

Embrace the Challenge

do: At the bottom of this page, here (he wrote a letter) *is the N for negativity, (now) give me a number."* I said, "OK, 1,000." He did something similar at the top of the page, adding a "P" for positivity. "Ok," he said, *"what's your number?"*

Suddenly, I understood everything, saying, *"Ohhhh, wow, 10,000. I know I have way more positivity then negativity;"* I was laughing as I said this. He then asked if I was interested in his answers, and I quickly agreed that I was. He said there was only one of each, and put the 1 beside each of my numbers. And, then, he began to draw, first a straight line down the centre of the page, and some wavy lines crossing the centre line and ending near the letters, N and P, until there was a picture of something that resembled a rollercoaster. He continued, *"It's either Positive or Negative."* He told me that I react like a rollercoaster, going high and then low, and then high again. It's better to choose your reactions more calmly and deliberately; one or the other. As you grow, you will manage to control yourself without making too much of a wave.

I had the urge to talk more about the reasons why I was unable to control my feelings, but I was aware of our time limitations, so I simply took a breath and asked him how he was able to do that in some, i.e., more disturbing, circumstances. *"You've been there, right?"* I added. He nodded, and warmly answered me, which caused me to sigh with hope for that level of control: *"I know that you're a Diamond, but this will only come when you can apply what Napoleon Hill called Emotional Control."*

Then he flipped the page and drew a tree with only a few branches. On the trunk of the tree, he wrote the word BLAME. Then, he drew some grass and a wave under the tree and added the phrase I AM RESPONSIBLE underneath. He explained that each branch stood for a word that meant negativity and, that each time I pointed a finger toward someone else, it was the same as cutting off a branch. He went on to say that I could cut the branches off one at a time (the usual reaction to the problem), but that probably wasn't the action I wanted to take because it wouldn't help the tree get healthier. Each time I cut a branch, or pointed my finger at others I was feeling negatively about, the tree was still sick. The right choice — the thoughtful choice — the most positive choice — would be to cut as far down as the trunk so the tree could start afresh. I left the meeting with a great understanding that this wise and humble man had just given me one million dollars' worth of advice within a mere ten minutes.

This wonderful analogy about responsibility and thoughtful choices took me a full year to integrate into my daily behaviour and, as I had been advised, I fell down more than a few times along the way. But, I continued to practice mastering my emotional rollercoaster to become more at ease with the correct posture and what I must expect when I choose to keep my bliss instead of losing my temper over something that's not worth it.

As I had achieved a Ruby level of leadership in March of the same year, I was included in the mentoring training retreat that I mentioned earlier. Our VP of Sales spoke, and what he said especially resonated with me as the timing was personally monumental. He gave an example about what to do when there is something huge to handle (like a business partner who is causing you problems) but you can't give the situation all of your time. He personally handled the situation by giving 20% of his timeframe to assessing the problem, and then used the remaining 80% of his time to have a real leadership conversation.

I came back home from that retreat and the convention feeling shaken by all the value and information I had received! It was the one-year anniversary of my dad's death, and I was remembering a lot of things about him and what he had said to me in the past. I finally understood that, for my whole life, he had been teaching me these lessons I was learning at last. But, because of the way I projected onto situations and held onto old wounds, I always came across as too emotional and my father saw that. I released the wound created by my father's judgments on this, realizing that he had said these things to help me protect myself from the ups and downs of my emotions. The analogy of the tree stays with me since that day. It taught me that life is all about how I choose to observe and interpret things in my life. If I immediately react, I may not get the result I want but, when I think my way through the situation and find the better way to respond, positive things can happen. There are lots of advantages to doing this, and I will share quite a few of them as we go along.

Embrace the Challenge

It's What's Under the Tip of the Iceberg That Counts

"What a person shows to the world is only one tiny facet of the iceberg hidden from sight. And more often than not, it's lined with cracks and scars that go all the way to the foundation of their soul."
– Sherrilyn Kenyon

When I achieved my first rank of leadership, it was an opportunity to train people in ways that I had never dedicated myself to before. I did it with blind enthusiasm and was there for anyone who needed me. I observed that what people were seeing when I stood at the front of the room – a leader – was what I had become because I was so involved in and dedicated to my own transformation.

Imagine an iceberg, and not just the tip of the iceberg, but all that lies below the water line. When seeing the iceberg in your mind, remember that three-quarters of it is below the surface of the water, just as there is always a lot of the work that needs to be done or things that need to be refined inside ourselves, if we are to be successful. It is that three-quarters of the iceberg that must be taken seriously and addressed with great personal responsibility.

Here are just some of the things that lie below the tip of the iceberg:

- Your risks
- Your focus
- Perseverance at different moments of huge discouragements
- The sacrifices you have made, like not seeing your family, investing money for training or to increase your learning and the time you dedicated to master those new skills
- How you aimed higher to visualize your big goals; all the actions/steps you took like working hard late at night or even during weekends; and how you kept going against all odds but never gave up

I am proud to have done all these things to become a leader. Most beginners took for granted that I was good on stage, looking up at me thinking "you got it" (meaning acknowledgement and a leadership position) easily, but nothing could be further from the truth.

Surround Yourself with Success

"Surround yourself with those who see greatness within you even when you don't see it yourself."
– **Zig Ziglar**

If you take a look at any high-powered leader, you will see that they have one or more mentors in their circle, and they surround themselves with people who are also successful. Today I surround myself with others who are committed to achieving their goals, and I work with several coaches and mentors who have taught me how to build rather than tear down. They are going to help me reach the next level and beyond.

Also, today, I choose to surround myself with colleagues and team members that are as committed to their success as I am to mine; more so, we are all committed to our mutual success without hurting the others. This represents a tremendous step forward for me as I used to choose saving and helping others – whether unconsciously or not – rather than myself.

So, I am supported. I have reconstructed my team of partners and mentors, and I focus on my purpose in life. I teach people how to have more meaning to their lives and to fulfill their dreams. It is imperative that we surround ourselves with supportive people who want the best us in an enlightened way.

Chapter 4

Give Yourself a Chance

"Those who succeed in an outstanding way seldom do so before the age of 40. More often, they do not strike their real pace until they are well beyond the age of 50."
– Napoleon Hill

As you can see, embracing the challenge, changing your attitudes, and building the self- confidence you need to achieve your goals and dreams is a process. You don't just snap your fingers and change overnight. I have been on my journey to a better self since I was 13 years old. And, today, I am a self-made woman who has raised the bar for myself by being aware that I had to change things from within. Of course, I had to take one step at a time, pulling away the layers until I reached the very core of each issue.

Don't get me wrong, I do not believe that everything about me had to change. There is great value behind my uniqueness, especially when you look at my loyalty, integrity, and sense of justice. I have always had a true desire to understand and defend those who are not in a position to express what they feel inside. I have also spoken out loudly in a lot of situations where I thought there was an injustice, only to be seen as a kind of Joan of Arc. Over the top? Yes, but it has served me very well in many instances.

Nor do I wish to suggest that my behind-the-scenes process is complete. Every lesson learned leads to the next lesson, and every change in behaviours needs to be practiced and refined. Plus, old habits can raise their ugly heads unless I am consistently vigilant about staying in a place behind-the-scenes where I can be aware of my perceptions and reactions and adjust my behaviours.

I have also engaged in so many battles and put myself on the front lines for others in the name of being recognized and appreciated, all because I did not feel of value. And, I used to be judged because I judged. These traits caused very bad consequences in my career. I now know to keep my mouth shut a little bit more of the time and to get my behind-the-scenes self out of the way of my own success.

These inner changes came about because of what I call my reconstruction. It's an ongoing process in which I have to find the faith to go back into a state of growth and pursue a path without being caught up by past reactions. That's how I put everything into place and how I began studying Napoleon Hill's laws and principles. As you can see, it's a process that has taken quite a bit of time, but it's also an amazing one that leaves me on the other side of each challenge I face.

Many of the lessons I've learned through this process are universal. They apply no matter what the challenge to be faced, and help me stay true to my path.

The Wounded Child

"Be who you needed when you were younger."
– Unknown

The child in each of us carries with it the hurts and fears that come to us as youths. We may think that we have moved forward from a slur, judgmental parents or a psychologically damaging event, but we usually haven't, and are likely to discover that, on many occasions, these past experiences resurface as part of our shadow side. When they do, there is an opportunity to heal this part of ourselves which we have had to repress.

The inner child stays within us and must be nurtured into wellness. In my memory, my childhood and young adulthood were filled with huge paradoxes. I was given so many gifts. We traveled quite a bit and were constantly stimulated with playful activities of all sorts. But, at the same time, my life was very structured, and I was compelled to do things when my parents thought I should do them, rather than when I wanted to do them — or if I wanted to do them. I was given my schedule in advance and was allowed no more than an hour of TV per day. There was a sheet of paper on the door of my room as a reminder to do my homework. And, there were restrictions of all kinds, such as when to go and play (when our friends were out and expecting us to join them), specific times for our extra-curricular lessons, and when our homework would be evaluated (we couldn't go out to play before our homework was approved by our parents). It's not that I was prohibited from playing, but the rigid lifestyle and my parents' high expectations for me made me feel that I was not being allowed to play. As an adult, I have recreated this level of perfection and it is what compels me to shut down my inner child so I can be an adult and keep working hard. (No wonder she wants to come out so often.)

I was an impatient child, always seen as screaming for no reason but, deep inside, I felt like my parents were just trying to shut me down. I felt they saw me as annoying, but all I wanted was to get their attention and to be heard and seen. Their reaction to my "screaming" imprinted on the adult me the (false) belief that I was always disturbing others. My parents wanted me to be very responsible and do what they wanted while, sometimes, I just needed to play more freely. I started to rebel, and reacted just as my inner child sometimes does when she demands to be allowed to play on her own terms.

Today, my innate child can laugh her head off (this is a particular gift of mine). One day, when my family was all together in my house, my four-year-old cousin, Clément, wanted to play construction. (He loves to play construction.) I started to show him how to fix something and grabbed a real tool in the process when he suddenly looked at me and earnestly shouted, *"But Dominique, we need the supervision of an adult because we are using real tools."* (There was nothing dangerous that could happen.) I answered him with the same level of authenticity, saying "I AM an ADULT." Everyone turned around and started laughing, especially me.

I am good with children; they love me because I treat them as if they were grown, and I ask them a lot of questions. I laugh and play fully just as they do because my inner child is spontaneous and passionate.

It wasn't always this way. I used to think, *Since I don't have success, I can't reward myself… I can't play.*

We all become our own parent at some level, projecting our parents' feelings and beliefs onto our adult selves. As such, we tell ourselves things that are no longer true, or lay blame when we do something of which our parents wouldn't have approved. I have learned to listen to what my inner child wants to tell me, and to give her some time to get what she needs. Then, once she has been given her place in the room, I can go back to work.

Now my inner child comes to me at various times of the day. And when I catch her repeating the voices from my youngest years, saying, *We must achieve,* and other unhelpful things that linger in my consciousness, I may give her my benevolent attention so as to keep those voices from sabotaging me in the moment. (It is her pain that can make me angry at someone when simple annoyance will do. It is her insecurity that takes things people say the wrong way.) As an example, I may allow her time to ache so I can then deal with a situation in a healthier way. I honour her feelings with more discernment than I did in the past, and I give her a treat afterward.

Acknowledge your inner child and fill him or her up – just as l do when I am painting and lighting up my heart. When I was taught to dialogue with her, I came to realize that being respectful of my feelings and expressing them are part of becoming a full person. If you don't do this, the wise child inside you may take opportunities to make you compulsive in your thinking – and in many areas of your life. So, if I hurt, today I say *"Ouch, this is hurting me"* or *"You are hurting me."* If I'm happy, I laugh, and everyone who sees me and has contact with me can see me being happy and authentic, just like a child.

Two weeks before writing this chapter, I saw myself doing something I had seen my mother doing, and I told her, with humour, *"Ah, this is where I get it from."* We laughed about it together. I love her so much, and we have both become successful at taking care of what we know about our little weaknesses. We talk a lot about our improvements and the acceptance of things for which we had a lack of tolerance. I can now see my mother for who she is, and I can call her on things that are upsetting. And, I can stop myself from doing those mirror actions that make me uncomfortable. We all resist seeing ourselves as our mother and father did and, as soon as we stop beating ourselves up and embody what is no longer a threat to us, reconciliation is possible.

The Seasons

"The strongest oak tree of the forest is not the one who is protected from the storm and hidden from the sun. It's the one that stands in the open where it is compelled to struggle for its existence against the winds and rains and scorching sun."
– Napoleon Hill

Nature is a great teacher for me, and serves as an analogy for many aspects of our lives. It is always in my consciousness. In the most basic and straightforward sense, the seasons represent the cycle of life. There is a time to sow and a time for what we sow to grow and prosper. Then, there is a time to reap the rewards of what has been planted, which is followed by a season for cleaning up the debris and another for preparing the soil for the beginning of a new cycle. Each of these seasons has its own weather; its own pluses and minuses. Think of the beauty and sense of hope that comes with spring and the first little weed to poke its head out of the cement. Then think of winter: cold, dark and inclement. During that time, we can find it more difficult to energize ourselves to go out and do what needs to be done.

At a deeper level, I use the seasons as an analogy in my life to detach from having an emotional response when it would be harmful for me to have one. We all go through cycles that mimic the seasons; sometimes we are in our own spring, energetic and focused, ready to act and achieve success. At other times, we may feel like it is minus 30 degrees and want to put our head under the covers. I cannot assume that someone is going through the same season that I am, and I have to detach from a situation when it is not working out. For example, I may be in my summer, feeling as if things should be happening because the sun is shining, but a colleague may be in their winter. I cannot react badly to that person's inability to be in summer with me. I must detach from my feelings and walk on.

Now, when it is raining inside me I know it is not going to last. Tomorrow, I may not feel the same way as I do today, especially if I nurture my inner child. Your inner weather is a way of telling yourself what you should and should not do, and whether you are in the right place to move your plans ahead. Are you trying to see something in the middle of the winter or are you trying to go against the wind? Neither will bring you success.

I was caught up in what I would call a cyclone last year. You know the type of storm I mean; it comes into a town and breaks everything. Cars go flying, buildings collapse, and a complete reconstruction is necessary when it's done. I experienced huge moments of turmoil, all pushing me to my last breath until I ended up completely burned out, exhausted and depressed. I was on the receiving end of slander and gaslighting, and shunned by some people on my team. The team's sense of unity was shattered and a partnership ended. But, I kept a smile on my face so, to this day, the other team members don't know the truth about what happened or why there is a distance between me and the team members who did me harm. Plus, at the same time, I was separated from people I had helped and loved, handling significant and ongoing problems with a tenant in one of my houses, had deals fall through on the house, had a major water leak in the house I was living in, dealt with aggressive neighbours, and more. Why did this happen? It was because I was still trying to handle everything by myself, not seeing that I was still resisting, still using my old pattern of fighting when I should have been letting everything go.

So, yes, not going with the flow is almost always a mistake. It's like going out without your umbrella and being mad because you're wet. I sometimes say to my partner that I am now more prepared for the storm; I have an umbrella in the car just in case of a sudden change, meaning that my boundaries (the umbrella) are in place to protect me. But, at the time, I thought, how can it be so unbearable when I am digging deeper than ever before to face my false beliefs of unworthiness?

The answer is that I had not been compassionate with myself nor had I given myself some time to heal the pain that comes from my resistance to taking off my protective shell. Realizing that, the more I felt angry about how slowly the transformation to my way of thinking was going, the more I prayed for my angels to stop it, once and for all. But there's no once and for all. Rainy days, storms, thunder, and clouds are still going to be part of the cycle. I know it's seems obvious, but getting caught up in my way of looking through the specter of the seasons gives me hope about what I will learn from it.

My mother used to tell me that I lived in my illusions and what could be called magical thought, which meant I had my own interpretation of things. If reality disagreed with what I wanted it to be, I was quick to maintain my view of things and to disregard good advice. Many disgraces followed because I fought the truth and didn't know what was in my control and what was not. (Again, going out in the rain.)

Before my journey, I let my moods affect me adversely all the time. If I had known to think of the seasons, I would have cursed over the weather all the time. Now, I use the weather and the seasons to inspire me, and to signal me when the time is right. Just as my cat would choose to stay inside and sleep on a rainy day, I may decide that reading a book or making phone calls is a better idea than going out into what feels like a stormy environment. Conversely, I may feel especially inspired to get out of my comfort zone when the season is right, like the grass that sprouts up between pieces of sidewalk in the spring or spreads out into the road.

So, when there is wind, just wait a bit for it to calm down. Even though there is darkness, you know the storm will end tomorrow. The sun will come out again, and it is the same for us. When you are in the midst of a storm, protect yourself, stay centred, and give yourself a chance. Especially in the biggest storms of your life, you must be your own best friend and protect your soul. And, for me, it is all about making the right connection between what is happening on the outside and inside. Don't try and force nature because it can't be forced. Look at the sea.

You should also look at what season and weather you are in when you meet someone. Try to look inside them as well. Are you synchronized? If not, it is not the right time to work with each other or for one of you to learn from the other. If you are overwhelmed, take a deep breath and the pause you need to regroup and become ready for the next step. There have been times in my own life when I was not in the right season to be producing results or attracting the right team members for me. If I had pushed myself too much, I would have made myself sick and still been unsuccessful. Although I wanted to reach certain goals, I had to give myself the space to calm down. I had to release the stress and be playful and laugh before I could enter a season of growth.

My sponsor, Michel Desjardins, talks often about his grandfather who worked in agriculture, and the metaphor is never lost on me. Just like a farmer, I plant a seed, and then I must wait for it to grow. It doesn't matter how passionate I am about that seed. It will not grow any faster than it can. Too many people want the harvest before they plant the seeds. They want to decide when the crops are ready, and life just doesn't work that way. I tell people now that I am at peace because I know that everything is perfect and that things will grow when they are meant to.

Reward Yourself

"Come up with a reward that you can use to motivate yourself."
– Unknown

If you are going to work hard, to do the kind of hard work that will make you a success, then you need to learn to enjoy the journey. Having balance in your life and playing hard are two ways to do that. Another is by rewarding yourself every now and then, perhaps with a spontaneous treat. When should you do this? How about when you do something exceedingly well, or when you reach one of your goals, or just because you put in 100% effort today?

Rewards don't have to be extravagant; sometimes a simple ice cream cone can make a moment seem special. So can enjoying a delicious gourmet meal, really taking in each taste and texture. I sometimes sleep in the morning after working a late night. It sounds simple, but it is rejuvenating.

I used to be so hard on myself that I couldn't give myself rewards along the way. I would literally forget to give myself a treat. Now, I buy myself a piece of clothing, and acknowledge the fact that what I'm buying is part of the rewards I am working so hard to attain. I also make time for meditation, walks outside, massages and other activities that allow me to pamper myself and regroup. I love the freedom associated with knowing I have been able to give myself something that gives me pleasure.

When we don't reward ourselves, we sabotage ourselves. I have learned this the hard way. If I don't get a weekend away, or do something else to reward myself every once in a while, the universe won't provide me with anything because I will be irritable or unable to accept those good things that I want in life. In order to attract balance and peace in my soul, I need to give those things to myself first.

How do you celebrate? Have you ever stopped working long enough to watch a movie in the middle of the day, just because the last few days have been difficult? Or, listen to a special piece of music, visit an art show or do something else that pleases your inner child or feeds your soul? The point is to keep your energy and hope up, no matter how hard a time it is for you.

Whether we are being amazingly successful or struggling, we all deserve the best. When life throws lots of tests our way, it is telling us that we aren't taking care of ourselves. Society is so focused on process and performance that is easy to forget about bringing joy and peace into our lives on a regular basis. We need to take that step away from the process every once in a while, in order to calm down. The more we celebrate, the more the universe will show us abundance.

Establish Boundaries

"You have permission to rest. You are not responsible for fixing everything that is broken. You do not have to try and make everyone happy. For now, take time for you. It's time to replenish."
– Unknown

By the time I came to write on this very subject, my original launch date for the book had passed. The book was supposed to be launched in May 2016 and my editor and I were far from what my goals had been. As I always say, when the lesson isn't yet learned, the universe shows us (ha, ha, ha.) Life definitely had a better plan for me. Remember the big plan?

I was trying to set boundaries, but I knew I had a hard time doing it. I once heard a colleague say, *"Dominique is always there to answer the phone at any time of the day."* When I heard that, I thought, *Oh my God, what am I doing to myself? I have to tell her that my schedule has changed just a little bit.* I said, *"If you want to speak with me, I now have to see if there is time on my calendar."* I wasn't being mean, I was learning to set boundaries, something I had not done by always being available. Now, I don't allow business people to call me on the weekends as that's when I recharge.

I kept trying to set boundaries with my associates but they were really and constantly pushing me beyond my limits. I used to make myself available for others until I was drained and resentful, often working from nine in the morning to ten or later at night. People asked too much of me, and I allowed it, trying to do everything for everybody; I was left vulnerable to my emotional past and exhausted. The pressure in my life was coming from everywhere (too much to explain). One day, when I was filling my pool, the pipes in my basement bathroom walls EXPLODED. Two hours afterward, there was water inside my walls and on the floor. This was a HUGE disaster and, of course, it happened on a Sunday night when nobody could come to fix it. Fast forward. We were obliged to open all the walls, the roof, and the floor to find out exactly how much damage had been done, only to finally declare that the whole basement had to be stripped and remade. Other major problems came from that broken pipe as well, and there was water almost everywhere: in the fireplace, dripping from the windows, in the bathtub and the shower – you name it, it had water in it. And I was crying and sobbing so much, that there were as many tears as there was water in the house.

I was paralyzed for quite a long period of time during which workers had to stop often as I was traveling to my trainings, camps and conventions, as well as a new program for which I had just signed up. So, the basement refurbishment weighed on my mind during a year's worth of endless problems related to my boundaries – all of this was happening at once! What could be a more perfect analogy of being brought to the floor again?

All that was going on was a sign that compelled me to take time to continue and write my book, as well as to do a lot of other things to reconstruct my entire foundation. I am so grateful today because I wouldn't have crossed the path of Marcia Wieder and I wouldn't have completed her full year program at "The Meaning Institute" if my book had been finished in time to make the original launch date.

Now, guess what? I set boundaries to make sure that situations don't sap my strength and that there is enough time to recharge my energy and power. If you do not respect my boundaries, you will not have my respect. Nor do I get involved in other people's personal drama – I just don't have time for it anymore. If your life is tumbling down upon your ears, I can't allow myself to be dragged down with you. I know the cost of it! What I can do is teach you how to help yourself and how to create the possibility of stepping into greatness rather than despair. So, yes, I can show you how to be free but, beyond that, I will not go.

I trained myself to establish a spiritual balance and to reframe my boundaries around what keeps me centred. This too was a major step forward.

Play Hard

"Surround yourself with people who take their work seriously, but not themselves, those who work hard and play hard."
— **Colin Powell**

Since you are reading this book, it is likely that you, too, have made the choice to fill your days with hard, enjoyable work. As I mentioned above, you must balance that work with personal time, and to do that effectively means taking the same focused approach to your leisure time that you do to work. This goes beyond the occasional treat you give yourself.

Play hard. Ask yourself what you loved to do as a child that you have given up in order to be an adult. Visit somewhere you have always wanted to go or, if you love sports, make time to play them on a regular basis. The statement, "Whatever the mind of man can conceive and believe it can achieve" by Napoleon Hill does not just apply to work!

So, what would you choose to do if you didn't have to work 9-5? What are you looking forward to having the time to do in retirement? Make time to do those things now. Live your life, don't just work at it!

Create Your Own Balance

"You have to learn to understand the waves and rhythms in your life and to live within those rhythms in order to be in harmony with the world."
— **Napoleon Hill**

When I say work hard, play hard, I don't mean to do each or both of them until you fall apart from exhaustion. Without balance, you lose perspective, and things can get blown out of proportion. Your body may signal you to slow down, either through illness or accident. You may deplete your resources, both emotionally and physically, by filling up every possible moment in a day. It can get to the point where you aren't able to enjoy your life.

Give Yourself a Chance

It's not just a matter of treating yourself well or taking a break. Your time needs to be evenly apportioned to work, sleep, family, and personal things (including spirituality). If one of these areas is not properly looked after, the others will suffer. It's really that simple.

Ask yourself these questions: What is a perfect day for you? What is the perfect week? What do you need to nurture your spirit and body? Also, watch for the signals your body sends you; perhaps you are suddenly getting headaches every day. Identify your own needs first and schedule time on your calendar to meet them. And, now knowing how important balance is, be aware of others' needs to create peace of mind and honour them.

Chapter 5

Change Your Habits, Transform Your Life

"Too many of us are not living our dreams because we are living our fears."
– Les Brown

As you have now seen, I came to understand that my old ways of thinking, my need to be overly protective of myself and my beliefs, and my need to always be right made me a person who was constantly reacting to what was happening around me. The result of this thinking is that I did not always take the time to understand the story behind what was being said or done to me; I just reacted in the moment. I put the blame on other people rather than admit I was less than perfect, and could be partially responsible for what was happening. In other words, I could see only my side of everything, never stopping to look at a situation from the other person's point of view. I lashed out at others rather than thinking through each situation, and what might come as a result of my words or actions. Again, all of this was keeping me from being successful in both my professional and my personal life.

I came to see that being impulsive was something I had to change if I were to progress in my journey. You may have other habits, whether they be always running late, procrastinating or otherwise self-sabotaging, but this was one of mine. I have seen that being aware of my impulsivity and catching myself more often has transformed my life. I did not always do or say everything the wrong way, to be sure. It's just that I could not always judge my own behaviour. Sometimes, when I was alone with another person, I would be unsure about the way I had acted and worry that I had not said everything in a loving and compassionate way. At those times, I needed an outside person to tell me when I had done well, especially if the person I had been talking to had not reacted well to what I said, or had spoken inappropriately to me.

After a while, it is a matter of practice, of just saying things without any emotional charge, and in a respectful way that is aligned with who I am. I understand that if I am constantly careful about how I say things, it may transform how I am perceived. On a daily basis, it is about practicing communicating in a respectful way, even though I disagree with the other person or they are being aggressive or hard on me.

Stay Out of Your Comfort Zone

> *"Stretch your comfort zone. Your comfort zone is in direct proportion to your 'money zone.' Be willing to do what's uncomfortable. It's the only time you're growing."*
> *– T. Harv Eker*

When I was building my company, I realized that I was out of my comfort zone most of the time – and that was a wonderful thing. I am naturally a solution maker, which means by default that there has to be a problem to solve, and that often calls for treading on unfamiliar, and therefore, uncomfortable ground.

I would not have become successful if I had stuck with only those things and situations that were easy. How can we expect to be in a better place if we don't think out of the box? And, more importantly, if we don't actually stand outside of the box. Every person who reaches some level of success has had to walk on unfamiliar ground and step out of their comfort zone.

Because we are creatures of habit, it is tempting to go back to the couch and be comfortable when things are hard. But, in truth, there is nothing more gratifying (and ultimately more comfortable) than reaching another goal. Mentors helped me realize that this – being uncomfortable at first and then becoming comfortable with a situation, person or job – is essential to moving ahead.

Are you making an effort to step outside the box?

There's a great example of staying out of your comfort zone in this next topic.

Go the Extra Mile

"When you go the extra mile the Law of Compensation always reward you, sooner or later."
– Shane Morand

When you are totally committed to something, you will do whatever it takes to do it successfully. You will go to any lengths to achieve your goal, sometimes not knowing where your strength is coming from as you do whatever needs to be done. It is only after the fact that you realize you were transported by faith and your desire to go beyond what you thought possible when you started out.

In January 2014, I returned from my annual holiday, which had been delightful. As I had one foot in the door, my phone started ringing. It was my mother, saying that my father had been admitted to the hospital for recurrent cancer, and that he was expecting my visit quickly. She told me that we didn't really know how much time he had left. Holiday was over!

I was extremely anxious as I arrived at the palliative care facility. As they had mutually agreed, that is my father and his beloved life partner; my father told me that he needed to maintain a sense of normalcy, including his personal daily habits. This meant that my father was not expecting my brother and me to visit more often than usual, he just wanted us to keep to the schedule we had before he entered the facility. My father wanted his time to be with his beloved as he would be on a normal day. He was very explicit when expressing this point – he didn't want everyone to come all the time as it would be too stressful for him to bear.

For me, it became a little bit scary, because we knew he didn't have much time left to live but, as he explained, if we were to visit him too often, it would cause him to focus solely on his illness and that he was going to die extremely soon. But, if we kept to a more normal schedule, he would be able to have hope, and to believe he had more time – perhaps a long period of time – and possibly, even be able to recover. His saying all this showed me how strongly he retained his thirst for life and his willingness to nurture hope for healing. My father didn't accept even the tiniest bit of a chance that he was going to die, even though the doctors had told him he would never be able to go back home, ever.

At that same time, I was in a leadership position, working with other leaders of Quebec to help our Diamonds create our most important event. This required filling a room with 4,000 people, which is what needed to be done if we were to have the co-founder and VP of sales as hosts.

As you remember, my father was not a man who showed his feelings, so he was holding on to life fiercely, but with difficulty. Seeing my dad in this vulnerable position was really hard to bear. I could feel everything and, after I left his room that night, I sobbed all the way home. I felt scared and deeply connected to his pain. I was thinking, *OK, I've got to bring him hope and positivity, and good vibes.* As always, I was willing to support him and do my best to nurture his well-being. I came back a few days later, well prepared; I had my lunch and a bag with his self-published book of poetry (my father had written about his favourite topics, things he loved). I told him that he deserved to continue dreaming and be inspired instead of just facing the green walls of his hospital room.

I knew that having his book would stimulate my father's thirst for those things to which he had dedicated his life outside of work, and the many projects he still wanted to do. I dedicated all my heart to our time together and, at the same time, was going my extra mile for our business event, the date of which was getting closer and closer. I made conference and three-way calls without giving any excuses to my partners. I helped them and was more dedicated than ever.

For example, each time my dad fell asleep, whether it was after a meal, or in between those sacred moments I had with him, even after the hardest ones, I sent emails and made calls because I had to make this huge event happen! Even though my heart was breaking, and even though the most comfortable thing to do would have been to just stop doing and feel my incredible sadness, I had to find the focus and strength to make all the calls required to get people to come to the event. It was about giving my every ounce and reaching out to the people I was afraid to reach out to; these were not just regular cold calls, but calls to people who were significant to me.

I still remember my father's look while he was eating as I was reading to him. He was in a state of happiness and memory and, with his spoon suspended in the air; he stopped eating long enough to let out a whistle of one word, saying, "Continue." There were times that I stayed the whole night and, during those moments, I brought my work. I had a list of people to call and used my phone in the corridor, going back into his room often to see if he was OK and to hear him breathing.

The nights I made the hardest calls were also some of my most difficult ones with him. I was looking at a man who wanted to continue his life, but that was impossible. I knew I could not waste one more hour of my life. I owed this to my father, and I continued to make the supreme move of inspiring people who knew exactly what I was going through. I continued to give my presentations, conduct training, and talk to people (saying, *"I want you to understand that you have to fight for your life. My father is dying, but my life continues."* I could have cried and hidden in my bed but, no, I went my extra mile for that event. We have to take responsibility, to make it happen.)

One evening, as I was reading him a passage in his book, the one he wrote about his life's path, my father confided in me, talking about one of the turning points in his life. He said, *"Dominique I know when my cancer started: 40 years ago."* He had been fired from a good position when my brother and I were young children, and he could never accept it. My father told me how resentful he was and how he had never forgiven them. It was this that had poisoned him. I was there listening, lightly touching his hand as every part of his body was painful. And, then, he stopped and said these words to me. *"You are the very essence of happiness for a father who gives rise to a child."*

I told my father, *"Dad, we should write it down before I forget and to be sure I really heard this coming from your mouth."* We laughed. As I had nothing to lose, I opened myself up to my feelings and this time I said, *"Dad, I need you to know that it is very interesting how life may surprise us at the very moment we expect it the least. You said things to me that make me understand why you couldn't give me any of the acknowledgment I was craving from you. I had to learn it for myself and gain back the understanding that I am the only one who has to be proud of me because it's a matter of perception. I have made assumptions based on behaviour, and I thought you rejected me, especially because you never expressed your approval. And, I have given you all the blame for my misinterpretation. Tonight, you gave me the acknowledgment that I have healed by my own achievement and by my reactions today, and my wounds no longer hurt."*

I continued, telling him, *"I want you to know that I am grateful for the gift of what we have been in each other's lives, with you as my teacher because you really have played your role to perfection. And I have played mine. Today I receive the most beautiful compliment a child may receive from his parent, and I wasn't expecting you to be proud of me anymore. I am healed, and I know how hard it is for you right now, but I am here. You can count on me. I love you."* He had tears running down his cheeks, as did I, but those tears were filled with compassion and real unconditional love. I said to my father. *"I don't want you to worry about me. Everything is fine."* He then shared with me, *"You really understand everything, your reflection is so complex and deep, I think I understand what you mean."* Then, he opened his emotional side up for the first time and spoke in my language, saying that I was the only person he had worried about and that he had been hanging on because of it. *"But,"* he said, *"now I know I can rest and leave."*

The day before we had this amazing conversation, my father had been told that he could probably be moved to another hospice, with a better quality of life, as he had seemed to recover a bit. My event was just a few days away, and we had sold almost all the tickets. I had a last training that was very important to me as it was the first such training to be held in Montreal. So, I said to my father, *"Dad, don't worry. I am busy with my business and close to reaching my next level of achievement."* I really was excited about the event and left that night thinking he would be transferred the next day. Just as I got to the special training session, I received a call from him on my cell phone. He told me, *"I am waiting for your next visit."* But, that proved not to be the case.

It had been a transformational month for my father and myself as we covered so many things that we had never been able to before. But, our conversation that night was the very last one we would have in which he had his mental facilities. In the last two days of his life, he was in a coma. I still read him poetry. And, I ate my lunch while reading him a passage from a book that explained what he could expect to celebrate on the other side of the veil. My father's dying produced a profound healing, as I had the privilege of being with him the night of his death, along with my brother and my father's beloved wife.

Our event ended up being the biggest one ever in the entire direct selling industry in Canada, and I celebrated heartedly while my father was already in a coma; he died two days later. I received my Ruby leadership rank in Rome at the first European convention a month after my father died. When I was spending time with my dad and meeting my business responsibilities at the same time, I was going the extra mile. It's about doing what it takes to make things happen. What new actions are you willing to take to receive the changes in your life that you are waiting for? Commit to doing what it takes – and all of what it takes – to transform your results.

Stop Pleasing Others

> *"If you aren't in the arena also getting your ass kicked, I'm not interested in your feedback."*
> *– Brené Brown*

You need to stop pleasing others at your own expense. I used to give other people all the credit way too much of the time, just so that they would love me. And, I was complimentary to others even when I wasn't being truthful (telling little white lies). I was equating being loved with being respected, and I was mistaken. Having people love you is one thing; having their respect and being successful is another. Plus, you simply cannot please everybody. I learned this the hard way.

It was my mistake to stay in places and situations where my desire to make a difference was unappreciated, sometimes to the extent that I bothered and annoyed others. Then, when my input and actions were not warmly received, I ended up seeing myself as other people's victim. Instead, I should have believed in myself and my willingness to take positive action. I should have taken in all the good and been my own best friend.

Pleasing yourself first also means taking care of yourself and making yourself happy. I gave everything to others, especially my time, putting myself and my needs last. There wasn't sufficient time to rest or play. And, this led to some bad habits. For example, I tended to arrive late to everything because I was doing too many things at once. It also meant I didn't take the time or rushed through the things I love to do.

These past two years, adversity was an unrepentant mirror. I couldn't understand why I was stuck in situations that I found unacceptable. From my point of view, other people were constantly deciding where I would be or not be, and I resented it. Looking back, I can now see things a bit differently. It's not that people ordered me, but rather than I let them make the decisions without saying a word. And, if those decisions meant I was to be excluded from something, I felt left behind and reverted to my old habit of shutting down. The point is, I was pleasing them and not pleasing myself.

I saw that I had to take myself and my resentments out of the way and, in a respectful way — without fighting — just take my place where I knew I needed and wanted to be. That applied both physically and emotionally. I also needed to reserve some of my time to regenerate my strength and power and re-centre myself so I was aligned with my own heart. And, I had to stop comparing myself to or pleasing others just because they had inspired me at some point.

I also used to become completely irritated, frustrated, and angered each time I saw someone giving themselves the right to certain behaviours that I couldn't allow myself. Why could they please themselves when I couldn't do the same thing for me?

After all my inner work trying to understand why I was in the position I was, I realized that adversity was back in my life again to such a large degree because I had been lacking self-respect. It was so unbearable for me. And, things didn't begin to change until I retracted some of the nonsense I had put out there and started being my own best friend, honouring my own being, finding balance, and pleasing myself before pleasing others.

Don't Try to Change Other People

"Don't make someone a priority when they make you an option. You are the value."
– Edwin Haynes

Fearing rejection by others, I often tried to bend their will or transform their beliefs and actions to be in line with mine. The thought was simple: if I could change them so that they would agree with me, then I could win their approval. This may sound contradictory to other things I've been saying, but it is just another side of the same issue – needing to be loved and right. When I couldn't change people or their opinions, my emotions, anger, and reactive nature would emerge at full strength. Now, on a daily basis, I practice communicating in a respectful way even though I am not in agreement with the person I'm speaking with, or the person is aggressive and hard on me. We must be careful in how we speak and act toward others because what we do will come back to us. We don't have to play their game.

There are many battles worth waging in life, but a battle not worth fighting for is the one over a certain point of view.

Today I know that the only person I can change is myself, and that what I have to change is my perception of the situation. It is important to understand that I can be right, and feel good about being right, even when the other person has a different opinion as to what should be done. They don't have to agree with me, for me to feel good about myself. And, when they disagree with me it doesn't always mean they don't like or respect me.

Change Your Mindset

"Every man is what he is, because of the DOMINATING THOUGHTS which he permits to occupy his mind."
– Napoleon Hill

It's likely you have seen something like the title of this section before, but it is a universal truth that has helped me through the most stressful of situations. When you are in the middle of something stressful, or an unexpected negative situation, think of it as a storm. Be the eye of that storm! It is critical that you stay in the moment, remain calm, and focus on what is truly important. As an example, the year before I wrote this book was one of great adversity for me, beginning on the 8 of March 2015 (International Women's Day). At the time, I was very happy to be back on track in terms of my career and my growth. Also, as a reward for all my hard work, I had signed up for a training program I had found valuable in the past but hadn't been able to attend for the last eight years for economic reasons.

Then, on the eighth, I came home to find I had been robbed. The front door was open, and the first thought that came to me was *Where is my cat?* In an instant, I was back in warrior mode, trying to see what was going on with my kitty. Despite the stress of the moment, I knew that everything else was replaceable. The experience was a huge reminder of what is really important in life. I stayed focused and was able to be happy because my cat was there and unharmed, not much was broken, I was alive, and it all could have been much worse.

I also managed to stay calm and focused in the aftermath of the robbery. My computers had been stolen, which meant that I was going to have a very difficult time with my taxes. I was going to have to do them manually and, because of a recent move into a new house, I couldn't find any of the hard copy files. I even had some aggressive neighbours who tested me a lot. All this, one thing after another, was unbearable. Yet, I made a decision to resist my old way of looking at things (me as a victim), kept my head up, and continued walking my way. I told myself, *"It's all going to be okay, Dominique. This is all happening to help you change your way of perceiving things. You can have dignity and cope with what's happening."*

However, I still had a long way to go. I had to make a huge change in how I interpreted what was happening to me in any given situation. Today, instead of focusing on what is not there, or worrying whether or not I have support, I change my perception to focus on the positive and the possible.

Let Go of the Story

"The other fellow's mistakes are a weak alibi for your own."
– Napoleon Hill

One of the very best things I did to get my power back was to let go of the story I was telling about myself. I became a force to be reckoned with. I quit pointing my finger at others and stopped blaming them for what was wrong in my life. I took responsibility for my poverty and decided to make my new story about being financially free. And, now I am. It took six years of very hard work, of becoming someone different. Six years of telling a new story and killing the old. But, I have done it. I have let go of the story of who I used to be, and now I live in the moment. And, I live in my power. And I draw on the wisdom of all my years. That is my new story.

The story that has wounded us can't totally disappear but, the more we nurture ourselves spiritually, the more we grow and the less the story can overwhelm the rest of our lives. We can change the paradigm, develop resilience, and express gratitude for all that has changed since the story happened. I learned to face the different parts of my story, to look at them and dialogue with them and then let them go. I continue to move past my story on a daily basis. When it pops into my head and starts to cloud my thinking I put it on the shelf.

Resilience and gratitude have to be part of the story!

Once you really embody the whole prospect of who you are as a human being and have tamed your dark side (which will continue to show up every once in a while), you will be able to go forward.

Now, let me ask you a few questions: Looking back, what has your story taught you? What benefits have come from the pain you experienced?

Are there parts of your story that allow you to play "little" or smaller than you really are as a reason to let your story be a challenge? What is your survivor mode or protective shell? What has given you the strength to carry on in the past but doesn't serve you anymore? Do you keep the pain of your hurts alive so you can replay them time and time again? Or, do you allow your wounds to heal and take responsibility for overcoming habits and behaviours that are no longer useful? What do you nurture? What breakthroughs have you had? What words of wisdom do you have that can help others?

Stand Up and Speak

"Courage is what it takes to stand up and speak. Courage is also what it takes to sit down and listen."
– Winston Churchill

It took a truly unbearable betrayal for me to jump into a greater place, one in which I just had to stand up for myself. Before that time, I was often fearful that taking such an action would cause people to dislike me or, worse still, disrespect me to an even greater degree. As much as I was always putting myself on the line for other people I believed I had harmed, I was horrible at doing it for myself.

Overcoming your fear of confronting people who are disrespectful is essential to serving family, community, and even humanity as a whole. We must all respect ourselves and our opinions, and not just when we are alone. It is crucial to stand up for ourselves in front of other people. I have also come to understand from my own experiences that not doing so hurt me physically as well as emotionally. Very often our bodies cry out when our mouths cannot speak.

When I started to change my behaviour in this area I did not do it perfectly. At first there was a lot of crying and rigidity on my part. I ruffled a lot of feathers and hurt a lot of feelings, but that was never my intention. Part of my journey has been learning how to refine the way I stand up for myself. I sometimes still raise my voice, but controlling it and being accurate are the better ways to respect who I am.

Stop the process of being a victim and stand up for yourself. Handling our emotions is the best way we have to be able to control the conversation, even if it turns difficult. I was in a delicate situation with a real estate agent not long ago, while I was still having to handle the woman who was renting my house and not paying what she owed. My interactions with the real estate agent put even more pressure on me and, instead of being helpful, she misinterpreted me constantly. On many occasions, she made some very harsh comments and I really had to practice what I was going to say to her before I said it. Still, she was disrespectful to me. I tried being cordial, smiling and handling myself with complete composure, but the time came when I had to stand up for myself. I ultimately told her to leave my house, which was something that had to be said. When you are good at telling a truth that the other person doesn't want to accept, they may behave badly because it is their only way of addressing something uncomfortable. But, you cannot let this keep you from standing up for yourself.

Chapter 6

Stop Lying to Yourself

"It is only when you're lying to yourself that you'll get an emotional charge from someone else's behavior."
– Debbie Ford

The world is a mirror through which we can see our actions and reactions. We must be honest about what we see there and consciously adjust ourselves if we are to move forward in our lives and achieve success. Be aware of which things prompt you to be reactive and emotional. Do you hold on to resentments? Especially, when you are failing to get what you most desire? If you do, the world is showing you it is time to change.

Letting go or easing my ties to the most painful of my roots has proven to be the answer to my problems. There were a lot of things I had to let go. I let go of my false beliefs and my willingness to be right at all costs. I was too proud and too insecure at the same time. And, I have had to let go of trying, as I do, to change how some people see me. Are you aware of the things that you must let go of because they are not supporting you? And, do you know that you probably have many of them?

Of course, it took courage to stand up and transform my life. But at the age of 45 I loved life too much to be sitting in a living room watching TV and not having the lifestyle I deserved. We need to stop lying to ourselves! For me, it was about gaining my real voice back as I expressed my needs without justifying them. I stopped saying yes when I meant no and took the time to first find out how I felt before answering. I also ceased agreeing with someone right away, especially when agreeing with them would only meet their needs. Now, I really honour and protect my new rhythm before I step into another person's shoes. And, when I feel emotional, I allow myself to be vulnerable, and I share what I'm feeling as an invitation for others to become supportive.

Respect your own values and keep them in agreement with your words and actions. Be true to you. Say what you mean and mean what you say. Keep your word as if it were law, have integrity, and do your best. (It takes practice to show our true nature when we have worn a mask for so long because we were afraid that we would not be accepted as we are.

What habits do you have that don't serve you but, out of laziness, you continue to do? I have been compelled to do self-destructive things and I've gone from one addiction to another in an attempt to free myself from each destructive habit. When I stopped taking drugs at the age of 26, I didn't wait to be told that I needed to stop. I quit right away. Then, at the age of 37, I quit smoking because of my husband Miguel. I did that in four weeks after huge preparation, during which I put in place a sequence of follow-up actions in case I failed, but I didn't allow myself to do so. I exercised or listened to music each time I felt the urge. I had known that it wasn't going to be easy, and I reached out for support. And, I planned it all on my own, without telling anyone else, because I didn't want the pressure. I succeeded at these things, but they were huge and very difficult to overcome.

It is a great thing to overcome your own lies, and it gives you great pride when you do. So, take a hard look at your life through the mirror that is the world around you. And, if you don't like what you see, let go of the story that is keeping you there, and get support if you need it. There are so many beautiful ways to stimulate a new good habit that makes us proud to embody our truth. I did, and the results are amazing.

Stop Lying to Yourself

Attitude and Personality

"It isn't defeat, but rather your mental attitude toward it, that whips you."
– Napoleon Hill

I have spoken earlier in this book about my attitudes and the ways in which they held me back. I used to tell myself that the world had wronged me and that my disappointments were all the results of other people's actions. As I've told you, I was the victim and other people were the villains in my life. Things had been done to me. People would not act the way I wanted them to and some of them were holding me back. I thought that these were the things that were keeping me from finding my greatness. I was too good, not good enough, or bad. I was wonderful, I was tortured, I was meant to remain a poor struggling artist. I told myself these lies for so long and, the more I repeated them to myself, the more I believed them.

Of course, I did not suddenly wake up one sunny morning and say to myself, *"Time to work on my attitude."* I had to first become ready to change them. I had to go back and examine how I was allowing my roots to continue getting in the way of my happiness and success. I had to see myself as a winner and step into my greatness. I had to stop blaming others, especially those who had harmed me in the past, for what was wrong in my life.

By changing my point of view, I was able to embrace my personal power and abilities. In short, I had to see myself in the mirror that is the world, and believe that I was capable of stepping into my greatness. My prospects changed dramatically when I adopted a winning attitude and allowed my personality to shine; I am still very direct, very me, without being too aggressive or confrontational (at least most of the time, ha, ha, ha).

There are, of course, good parts to my personality. I am, by nature, empathetic and a woman with heart. I usually have a smile on my face and fun in my heart. And, as you can see, from the recounting of my survival during some terrible experiences in life, I have courage as well.

I care about people, and want to help them succeed (if they, too, truly want to succeed).

Let me give you few examples of what I had to refine at my starting point, during which I was listening to the audio of *Napoleon Hill*. (Each time I drive to a meeting, or elsewhere, I listen to audio books.) When I reached the chapter on "Assembling an Attractive Personality" this time around, I thought: *OK, wow* and laughed. *Bullseye! I got that right!!!* But, whoops. Later, when I got the book out again and started to study the section that had hooked me in the car, I found myself slowing down the pace as I started reading a huge list. I began to evaluate the positive factors of a pleasing personality. Let me be vulnerable here – and let's laugh just a bit!! I mean the title of the chapter alone! Here are just some of the things on the list:

- A Positive Mental Attitude....*And it started so well*
- Tolerance ....*WHOOPS*
- Flexibility.....*WHOOPS*
- A pleasant tone of voice...*hum...depending, if I am stressed ....hummm, WHOOPS*
- Tact ... *What is that? WHOOPS*
- Control of facial expressions ...*WHOOPS, gotta work on that one too!* I am a really an open book and when I felt something unpleasant you could tell, even though I tried to hide it. My energy was palpable (ha, ha, ha)!
- Control of temper and EMOTIONS (ha, ha, ha), *WHOOPS*
- Patience ... *I don't have time for that* (ha, ha, ha), *WHOOPS* I thought, *should I close the book at this point?* (ha, ha, ha)

OK, I thought, *breathe in, breathe out!* Of the 19 items listed, I had to adjust a couple of them and put lots of LOVE into mastering those important skills! They were of capital importance. And, yes, I am making jokes, but it is to show you how I am able to laugh at myself, especially when I am focusing on the things I don't do as well as I would like to. And, here I am talking all about the negatives without mentioning my positive attributes (of which there are many on that list just saying ha, ha, ha).

It is hard to change ourselves. To unleash a "persona" as huge as our "Controller" or "The Victim" or "The Perfectionist" – and these are just a few examples of archetypes I have been learning about with Marcia Wieder – we have to stop judging and give ourselves a chance. It is often just a matter of doing our best, as we all embody those types of personalities at different levels. They are deeply anchored.

I can assure you, the universe has provided the perfect people and situations for me to catch up and begin the real transformation. Do you relate? What kind of similar contexts has life pushed on you to unclothe your unpleasant personality?

I want to take a moment to introduce you to the well-known "Four Agreements" created by Don Miguel Ruiz. They represent a fundamental part of my growth, and they can help you, too, to achieve the success you deserve. When you read them, you will think that they are simple, but they are clear and wise guidelines; their strength is in the clarity and simplicity with which they lay out their meaning and purpose:

The Four Agreements

1. Be Impeccable with Your Word
2. Don't Take Anything Personally
3. Don't Make Assumptions
4. Always Do Your Best

Let me tell you how my awareness of these agreements put life into perspective when I was lacking integrity for myself but, at the same time, practicing to be at my best and trying to stop taking myself so seriously.

I have been very sad and ashamed on many occasions during my process of learning when I had to apologize for my words. I was searching for any good tips or information that I could use to help me correct those weaknesses and bad habits. To this day, "The Four Agreements" are my commandments, and I constantly remind myself about them or refer to them whenever I feel caught in a judgmental, vicious circle. It is so important to learn how to apply them in our everyday lives. And, we need to practice them over and over again.

The Turning Point

"No one can make you jealous, angry, vengeful, or greedy; unless you let him."
– Napoleon Hill

We all have to go through our turning points; mine was my divorce. Out of every turning point comes tremendous learning about how and why we feel and react in the present. We have to see where we are (or were) dissatisfied and do something about it.

I had wanted my husband Miguel to give me the acknowledgment, respect, and love that I did not feel my father gave me when I became an actress. I had to acknowledge that I was looking for the love I couldn't give myself. And, if I couldn't give love to myself, how could I expect others to give it to me? I knew all of this – and yet I felt trapped in my cage. The universe sent me signs while I was going through my personal turning point, and I made major decisions based on those signs.

What big decisions have you made to bring your life up to the next level?

Despite the things that brought us to the point of divorce, Miguel and I have been able to stay lovers and friends for eight years. We still exchange news and see each other every once in a while. I think that part of the reason we are able to stay so close is that I focused on myself after the breakup and didn't look at his part. This was a true turning point for me as it marked a time of self-examination. A turning point reflects our need to deal with circumstances and situations that rock the very foundations of our lives. It is the time to take a true inventory of ourselves, and decide which things, feelings and behaviours need to be cleaned out of our lives so there is room in our essence for our assets to grow and flourish.

Respect Others

"If you truly love someone, your love sees past their humanness."
– Michael A. Singer

Believe it or not, I succeed at letting others follow their own path and be themselves (ha, ha, ha). When I stopped judging who was good or bad based on my own point of view, I was free to make my own life what I wanted it to be. I chose to work with people with whom I have mutual trust and respect, and my soul is peaceful. This past year, the universe tested me yet again and I didn't understand how to recover from hurtful behaviours and slanderous statements made about me. I know that I have to forgive those involved and let the universe be in charge of the results. My intent now is to respect myself and to be able to respect others. This is how I master "The Four Agreements" and, keep myself from walking around like an automaton or going back into my ego mode, of which I have had enough. That being said, I have got to loosen up my longing to bring justice everywhere I go.

Do you respect others as they really are, especially the important people in your life?

Before I realized I have to accept and respect others for who they are, I often got irritated with either an associate or my brother who, as an example, does things very slowly. Let's say, the phone would ring while I was in a rush and, instead of letting it ring, I would feel compelled to answer; that is, to put the needs of the person making the call ahead of my own. When the caller was my brother, I would get especially impatient because I knew I didn't have time for a long and slow conversation.

Then, at an "Enlightened Warrior Camp," I was taught that the way I treat others shows them how to treat me. I have to respect others if I want them to respect me — and to respect my needs at the same time. So, now, if I don't have the time or space for someone else's needs at the moment, I know it is okay not to answer the telephone. Not only is it okay, it is my responsibility not to answer the telephone (rather than taking the call, sounding frustrated or angry, telling the person, "It's not a good time," and rushing to end the conversation).

Do you sometimes answer the phone while you're eating? Do you stop and talk to the person while your meal gets cold? That's what I was doing, thinking the call was going to be short, but it was not. Is it the same for you? We are the ones who set our own rules! This year I vowed to respect myself and others and, as a result, today I have much better relationships with people; and they now come to me in a more genuine form of attraction because I have become at ease with kindness.

My relationship with my brother and my mother is transformed because of these changes. When I coach someone as a partner or as a client I start by asking what they would like to change, rather than immediately telling them what needs changing. I tell them what I see needs correcting in their behaviour, not because it is bad, but because it is not serving them anymore.

Sometimes we give to others the things we haven't received in life. My craving for acknowledgment has wounded me, but it has also made me a master at the gift of being able to acknowledge others. During the years that I was presenting to teams and leaders, I always edified the people who had helped me build my business, as well as my partners. I used to thank people everywhere I went, expressing my gratitude and empowering them to make more and better efforts. Thank yous and compliments can come in the form of little things, but they mean a lot to people. I became aware of how powerful a tool this is.

I was given a card at the "All Your Relations" seminar with T. Harv Eker that lays out "The Seven Principles of Acknowledgment," written by Judith W. Umlas. I invite you to take a moment as you read them so you may realize their impact and recognize that they are a powerful tool for creating team-building or a need to consolidate fellowship. We may need to adjust our behaviours accordingly.

Stop Lying to Yourself

The Seven Principles of Acknowledgment

1. The world is full of people who deserve to be acknowledged.
2. Acknowledgment builds intimacy and creates powerful interactions.
3. Acknowledgment neutralizes defuses, deactivates and reduces the effect of jealousy and envy.
4. Recognizing good work leads to high energy, great feelings, high-quality performance and terrific results. Not acknowledging good work causes lethargy, resentment, sorrow and withdrawal.
5. Truthful, heartfelt and deserved acknowledgment always makes a difference, sometimes a profound one, in a person's life and work.
6. It is likely that acknowledgment can improve the emotional and physical health of both the giver and the receiver.
7. Practice different ways of getting through to the people you want to acknowledge.

Be True to Yourself

"Speak with integrity – Say only what you mean."
– Don Miguel Ruiz

There have been many times in my life when I wasn't being truthful to myself, as when I became the person other people wanted me to be or did things others wanted me to do, even at my own expense. In a real way, I was lying to myself by discounting my truth and always trying to please others. This hurt me, not just in my personal life but professionally.

No matter what the circumstances, be you. Do not bend your beliefs or break your own code of morality. Want what you want and know that it is the right thing for you. It doesn't matter if others think you should want something else, or that you should put their needs before your own. You may have to walk away from some of the people that you have worked with or befriended before, especially if they don't want you to be true to yourself, or if they cannot be there when you need them to be. Putting yourself first is more than okay; it is the right thing to do almost all of the time. Pursue your dreams and desires. Hold onto your beliefs, dreams and goals. Maintain your integrity.

A big part of being true to you is standing up for yourself and what you know is right. I owned a house which I had been renting out to a woman who was not paying her rent. I spoke with her time and again; still no rent. When we spoke, she was usually most disrespectful to me. It made no difference that I was totally in the right, of course, as her primary objective was to make me go away and stop asking for the rent which was due me. Now, I could have been disrespectful of the woman as well, but that would not have done anything good. Screaming and being hurtful would not have changed the outcome of our conversations; instead, it might have made matters worse. I stood up for myself but in a way that had empathy and grace. These new behaviours occurred right after my "Ultimate Leadership Camp" where I really took the time to prepare myself and to practice not getting angry (as she had been the one giving me reasons to lose my temper). It didn't happen! I reached out for support from the law and evicted her, but without being disrespectful (as she was). I was financially destroyed by the debt she put me in, but I have mastered the First Agreement completely with this women. She also will have to face the universe for what she has done.

Walk the Talk

"Integrity is doing the right thing when no one is watching."
*– **Unknown***

Who am I to be showing you the way? Someone who does more than just talk. And, more than just walk!

I am still on my journey, but I have already come a long way, through much perseverance and hard work. But, it isn't really enough to set goals and take the path to reach them. Often, people use the expression, "walk the walk." Many coaches and mentors say that is the hardest thing for most people to do. For me, I am already walking the walk, putting one foot in front of the other, working hard and dedicating myself to success. But, that's not enough. Having integrity is an integral part of walking the talk and I've held fast to mine, often raising my standards of what is right, rather than lowering them. To me, walking the talk means doing what I say and saying what I mean! Look where you are going in all areas of your life as you honour your word toward yourself and others.

I was not always this way. I did not always balance my words and ambitions with compassion for those who were less driven than I. I so wanted them to succeed that I bullied or pushed people who were not ready to share my sense of integrity and purpose, whether they were always late or lazy, or didn't do what needed to be done. Their goals may have been different than mine or, for some other reason, they were not ready for my path, but I kept pushing. Now I know that doing so was not good for them or for me. I should have let them choose their own path much sooner than I did. I should have let them walk their own path, alone, while I went ahead on mine.

Chapter 7

Who Do You See in the Mirror?

"In the process of letting go you will lose many things from the past, but you will find yourself."
– Deepak Chopra

Before I embarked on my journey to self-understanding and growth, I did not realize how much my thoughts and actions in the present where still related to the things that had happened to me in the past. The feelings of anger, shame, and self-doubt that surfaced when they were least helpful were firmly implanted in my thought and reaction processes. Those past experiences and the feelings they produce are the roots of my unease and self-sabotage. The only exercise I have been able to practice thoroughly is looking at myself in the mirror and, each time I face my image, telling myself I LOVE YOU. Most of the time, I couldn't stay in front of the mirror for more than a few seconds before I started to cry in disbelief of my words. But, I became more and more proud of my huge turnover to make myself my true nature of joy. I had to learn how to weaken the connection between my past and present feelings, to tug at or pull out the roots.

Roots

"Your outer world is merely a reflection of your inner world. You are the root; your results are the fruits."
– T. Harv Eker

The roots of my anger go as deep as those of shame and unworthiness. In the past, I would feel courageous for going forward, but I was not connected to the anger behind my courageous actions and I would push a lot of other people's buttons. When I upset those people, I did not receive the rewards I should have, especially the financial ones. Also, I have always given out millions of dollars worth of free advice and consulting wisdom (ha, ha, ha). How could I have expected money and gifts when I was giving my greatness away? I also constantly gave away money to those I thought were in greater need of it than I, so much so that I did not put funds away for the proverbial "rainy day." Again, I was taking better care of others to my own detriment.

The seminars I have attended, especially those over the last two plus years, have helped me see that there are layers to each of those feelings, and that I must approach each layer with compassion for myself. While I take responsibility for my past actions, I forgive myself; I respect myself and acknowledge that I can act differently once I have dealt with the roots of those actions.

I now see that I was not properly aligned to receive the rewards I expected. "The Millionaire Mind" seminar, which I have done more than once, made me aware that I believed myself to be non-deserving. That is, I did not attract money because, subconsciously, I did not believe I deserved it. And, underlying this lack of self-esteem was the anger I could not express when I was a child, as well as my long experience of being abused in all forms possible. The anger remained inside me and it has taken a long time, a lot of behind-the-scenes work, and a very upsetting financial experience to understand just how much I self-sabotaged through anger.

So, what have I learned about controlling this old anger when it resurfaces? In the moment, I look at what I'm feeling and ask myself, "Is this serving me, really? Is it helping me reach what I want or making me take a step backward? Can I bear it?" Afterward, I do an action that takes me out of the immediacy of the anger — whether it is acting, drawing, listening and becoming one with a piece of music or taking time to be by myself; sometimes when I'm alone I cry the feelings out.

Better still, sometimes I dance the anger out. It's about purging those un-useful feelings, and I have had to take these steps quite a few times recently, not just as I dealt with the court case involving the renter of my house, but also with others who were being disrespectful to me.

I also take myself through a process in which I become intimate with my anger. I ask myself more questions, often writing them down with my answers: What am I facing? What am I feeling? When and where have I experienced anger about a similar situation and what can I do to resolve my feelings about that earlier situation? Who is angry? Is it the child within or the adult woman that has been hurt? Allowing myself to recognize, acknowledge, and embrace the anger lets me set it free. And, I show myself the compassion I would give to someone else if they had acted out against an innocent person.

Keep Learning

"Experience has proven that the best educated people are often those who are known as 'self-made' or 'self-educated'."
– Napoleon Hill

I'm a student of life. I have always been one, someone interested in knowing more and understanding people better. Even though I still fail at the latter more than I would like, I am always authentic. And, I am always trying to spread the knowledge I have gained and listening to what others have learned. Being a student of life is not like going to school — you don't graduate. The more you learn the more there is to learn and process. This is what is true for me. This is my quest.

Not everyone feels the same way or understands the importance of continuous learning. People who are not as involved as I am in self-development or personal growth don't "get it." My father misunderstood my quest and was initially afraid that I was being brainwashed. He was especially fearful, although I tried to explain to him that I needed to be clean at another level. I told him that I had been destroying myself with drugs and that I was plagued with a lack of self-esteem. He didn't understand that I needed to learn how to break through the internal "stuff" to reach my full potential or that I also had to learn how to stand up for myself in a productive way, without harming innocent people. He was always saying that we already have everything inside of us. But, it's not what he said that counts, it's how he behaved toward me, which was in opposition to his words. My father's own facial expressions and non-verbal anxiety didn't bring me support. I had to go beyond what I knew he was thinking about all I had invested into developing myself further.

When you keep learning, you keep getting to another level of seeing and settling into your greatness. People often refer to this continuing growth as peeling the onion, because every layer you remove reveals new insights and instigates new changes for the better. The process is not about learning the same thing over and over again. It is about getting stronger and wiser with each layer, so you can continually reveal what's beneath when you are ready to take on the next set of challenges. This is true in all the areas of our lives.

It's important to choose your teachers and coaches carefully. They must walk the walk, not just talk the talk! I have seen a lot of people blindly follow a potential guru who, at some level, was preaching their wisdom, but was not totally applying their knowledge to what and how they were teaching. In a big way, those coaches were not good examples for me, and learning from them will be less successful for you, too, as opposed to working with someone who is aligned in talk and action.

For me, learning about money, physicality, health, and spiritually results in being congruent and aligned across all the aspects of life. It's all linked to serenity because, if we're not learning, we are inevitably going to repeat bad habits. (Don't I know it, ha, ha, ha.)

The phrase, keep learning, also applies to living and dealing with different kinds of people; knowing other kinds of behaviours and cultures allows for better and more productive relationships. In turn, that leads to reaching a greatness that comes when you receive, accept, and adopt what the universe wants you to learn. If you're not continually learning, the universe will send you lessons that force you to dig deeper. And, that is a great loss. I have finally learned how to have more discernment; that is to have more awareness of what mode I am in, spiritually and mentally.

Some people are very good at learning about the world around them, but shy away from learning more about themselves. If you are one of them, please ask yourself why. Are you afraid? Are your roots so entrenched, planted so firmly in the ground that you don't believe you can learn? Nothing could be further from the truth.

We must keep learning. We must continue to improve ourselves— for ourselves. We are in the time of a huge shift as everything goes fast and the universe waits for us to send it our message (yes, I have learned the lesson) so it can support us by sending the right people and situations into our life with synchronicity. When you are ready and ask, the universe will provide.

Do You Have a Vision?

"If you are working on something exciting that you really care about, you don't have to be pushed. The vision pulls you."
– Steve Jobs

I am asking you this, because, when I started my business I didn't realize the power of having a vision. I was aware of the concept but didn't really understand how transformative it could be. I did have a goal which, as I've shared with you, was to own my own home. I worked toward my goal, and achieving it took me from a point of ground zero to seeing myself as the proud owner of that house for precisely five years. That experience helped me understand the power of having a plan to work through the process, which starts with stating a desire and takes you through to the concrete manifestation of that desire. When I was asked to see and project myself five years into the future (as part of my first "Millionaire Mind Intensive" in 2007), it appeared too far off for me to envision where I wanted to be. But, step by step, I was brought to take actions on a daily basis and to keep going out of my comfort zone. I could take pages of my "90 Day Wealth Conditioning Program" by T. Harv Eker and show you how I visualized the exact house I wanted in 2007. Then, I could show you in a detailed way that the house I got was exactly as I wanted it to be, and how I got to the point where I manifested it in May 2012. Do the math!

But, I would rather tell you about "my why." I wanted my house because I had a burning desire to create my own little paradise, and my desire came true because of the investment I made in my company.

And, I assure you that I have followed the leaders of my company and Napoleon Hill's core values of helping others to reach their own dreams too.

If I had stayed in my little, wishful thinking state of mind, I would never have been able to buy this house. Having a vision is what gives you the power to overcome the things that are in your way and to find solutions along the way to make happen what you intend with a burning desire, no matter what. It is what keeps you focused and it makes you move around and above, under and below, when the universe sends you struggles to be overcome. And, it is in those moments that you see whether you are going to handle the things that require handling or if you are going to give up on your dream.

There is no doubt that setting off on a journey of discovery and transformation seems almost impossible unless you have a vision of what you want your life to look like, and make your own adjustment. I was tired of living in a poverty mentality that kept my success away.

Courage and Sacrifice

"Courage is not having the strength to go on.
It is going on when you don't have the strength."
*– **Unknown***

The universe has shown me on some other level that, if you are a leader, you have lots to master in terms of respecting yourself, even if others don't. This was a painful lesson for me. I invested my time and my soul in team members who did not turn out to be team players. I was tested, and for a while I was the loser of a battle I had not intended to have. Still, I found the courage to face the facts and look at the part I might have played in all the fighting so that I could be humble and grow from the unpleasant experience. Again, I came out the other side, smiling at all and not pointing my fingers elsewhere, because some of those players are still on my team.

If I want to have more success and reach higher levels of achievement in everything I do, I know I may have to step back a bit yet again and look at my own roots at least one more time. It doesn't matter how much healing or forgiving I've done, I may have to step up again. I will also need to stand on my own two feet and raise the bar again.

And, I will have to face my most recent failures with certain team members and believe in my own leadership because others have cast me aside for the moment. When you are on the field of battle and the enemy can see you dying, they assume that you are, indeed, dead. Little do my opponents know, I will rise again, stronger and more resilient than before. And, I will win because I choose to win.

There Are No Short Cuts

"Life has a way of testing a person's will."
– Paolo Coelho

My journey has been a long but incredibly rewarding one in which I had to take each step, one after the other. You will find this is true for you too. You don't just wake up one morning and find your life transformed. I've had many mentors and I have learned so much from each of them. I have taken seminars and courses and discovered something about myself in every one. Each time I gained wisdom from someone or something, it gave me the strength and willingness to accept the next lesson. This is how I have ignited my inner strength along the way.

I have always been a woman who does what needs to be done and goes the extra mile. When I was younger, the hard part was always knowing exactly what was needed. But, when I say I will do something, I do it (The First Agreement, "Be Impeccable with Your Word"). This is an agreement that I have made with myself. There are no easy, fast ways to do anything, be it in your emotional growth, business success or, well, anything in life.

Once, I was supposed to fly to St. Louis for our convention and to accept a qualification I had earned, as well as the privilege of being in the same group as others who had won it. This really meant a lot to me because each step up I achieved would bring me closer to the Diamond Circle, which is only for the masters who have reached that level of success. Being able to celebrate this achievement is capital!

There were at least 15 flights cancelled, including my connection flight. This made for a difficult situation. I heard people saying the next flight wouldn't be until morning, and I knew that if I waited for that flight I would miss the celebration. Right away, I knew that I would not let anything stop me. I didn't decide it would be too hard to get there and just give up and go home, or worse still, wait hours in the airport until I was pissed and complaining. No, I am not a complainer; I give harsh critiques, but I always find solutions instead of complaining.

It was midnight and all the hotels around the airport were full because of the flight cancellations, which had put hundreds of people in the same situation as I was. I rented a car, and drove to an expensive hotel (all the cheap ones were full by the time I had finished reserving the car.) I was with an associate at the time, Sophie-Kim, for whom I have great respect. I also appreciate her consistent loyalty. She didn't have extra money to cover the additional expenses all this caused, so I told her, "*I am the one who needs to be at the celebration. I'll hold my nose and deal with the financial issue and please be my guest.*" We set out at six o'clock the next morning and drove five hours to be at St Louis at the right time.

This opportunity became a huge footprint learning behind what I call today "There's no short cuts to achieve success in life." I shared with Sophie-Kim what I understood to be behind this long drive – the opportunity (and importance of) always doing whatever it takes to make something happen. Also, for me to learn that something which appears at first sight to be bad luck is put into my path by the universe for a specific reason – and that reason has wisdom behind it.

There are some important mistakes I have repeated over the years depending on who I wanted to help because I saw in them huge potential. These were people that couldn't come with me and assist at the International convention. I loaned money on different occasions, sometimes to ensure a qualification, or help someone start their business or even to buy their products. Doing this cost me a great deal, and the reasons behind my doing this "hit me" as I was driving the car.

When I loaned money to people who had not made the sacrifice and invested in themselves, I was offering up for free what I had worked so hard for, serving it on a silver platter. Not only did this put me in debt, it sapped my energy and made me resentful, especially as some of these people are not even involved anymore. They still owe me money, and keep making endless excuses without providing any kind of acknowledgment or thank you for the favour.

When you make life easy for those who find reasons to justify why they can't invest in their business or in themselves, it may only lead them to failure because you have given them a short cut and, in real life, there are no short cuts to succeed.

My reasons for doing what had to be done to attend this once in a lifetime reward, especially as I had achieved what we call a Ruby level of leadership that same year, brought out my determination and willpower. It took what it took to participate in what I consider a forever memorable afternoon with the Diamondship, and this privilege was due to my own efforts; it was truly a deserving celebration of success.

Build the New YOU

"Whatever good things we build end up building us."
– Jim Rohn

Courageous people are able to face their own failings, learn from them, and construct a better self from what they have learned. It is not an easy path to take, but it is a crucial one if you are to become the true, most powerful you. I have never been a patient person, but I have had to learn to be patient because building the new me has taken time. It is still happening. I am still constructing a more self-confident leader. I am still getting better at choosing the right people to work with and, perhaps most importantly, I am still learning that change comes over time; not just in me, but in the process of just about everything I do.

If I continue to learn, and earnestly do my own duty, I can build upon my strengths and improve my weaknesses, understanding that any behaviour that does not result in getting what I want and need is a weakness — at least in some situations. I have seen in my own life that, sometimes, being tenacious ultimately brought me great rewards. At other times, however, I held onto an idea or a person for far too long and was disappointed time and time again.

Last winter, I put my own process of success on hold because I needed to find the better way to reboot everything. Sometimes, the teachings of our past need to be revisited to unstick us from what I call residual old programming.

Today, I prefer to attract residual income, if you know what I mean (ha ha ha ha). There's nothing better than replacing the positive mental attitudes (the PMA principle of Napoleon Hill) I've acquired with improved ones, then seeing the results that come from doing so. And, at this point on my path, I better support who I am when I have to adjust, correct and continue. I give myself a pat on the back for noticing that my challenges turn up less and hang around for shorter periods of time than ever before. And, I am aware of the cycles of life, so I am more alert. What's important is now, when I catch my ego screaming, I may laugh at it and compel it to take a break. I am also continually aware of old thoughts when they arise and can allow myself to give them the briefest moment in time before replacing them with better beliefs and things I intend to create.

Be Your Own Leader

"Before trying to master others, be sure you are the master of yourself."
– Napoleon Hill

When you are a follower in your own life, you allow other people to make decisions that are not right for who you really are. They will choose what is best for them, whether they know it or not. They may even mean well, but no one can know your inner truth as well as you can. They can't know how courageous you are, or see into your heart to know your most important desires. When you continue to follow the advice of others, you are giving in to the fears and disappointments they have for you.

Who Do You See in the Mirror?

Do you want to continue following along behind everyone else? I needed to tug hard at my roots of anger and pain so that I could get in front of my life, rather than staying stuck behind. I did not have command of my own destiny, in that my actions allowed other people to make too many decisions that were not in my favour. And, as I've said, I allowed it to happen without saying a word.

So, do you want to follow other people's rules or the rules of the universe? Do you envision a better life for yourself? Do you see yourself as a leader, someone who helps others by example and by sharing your experiences?

As a leader, I enter into a partnership with the people I work with. Together, we define what they want to achieve and why. This is critical. If you are potentially a star, and are dedicated to doing the work, I can bring you along more quickly than someone who is not interested in reaching the same level of achievement. I was not always as good at listening to what people really want as I am now and, out of need, I put too much heart and energy into the wrong people. Choosing to work with people who were not sufficiently motivated provided me with additional opportunities to adjust my "communications skills," and I am grateful that I could see them as the opportunities they were. Plus, I have come out the other side.

Being a total follower in all aspects of your life won't make you happy. It won't give you self-confidence or build your self-esteem to the level where you can truly acquire those things you deserve. I want you to become your own leader in your own sense. It can be in your family or professionally; it can happen at one or more and different levels, perhaps even in more than one area of your life, but it must be in something that fulfills you.

Transforming yourself from a follower to a leader requires work; it requires practice. I now ask people what they think because it is important to have your own opinion. I always doubted my own self and was not able to make strong decisions on my own, which meant I let others get in the way of my conceptualizing and owning my own destiny. Now I see myself more as an equal to others, the real

Dominique who wants to share her vision, her passion, and her wisdom.

I could have not have talked or written about this subject even a few months ago. It is only because I continue to learn and grow that I am able to face these next layers of my onion. I have achieved greater skills because of the application of the principles of Napoleon Hill and other, newer teachers like Marcia Wieder.

Being the leader of my own life means choosing what is the right path for me. Only I know what steps must be taken along that path. If there is a fight ahead, I will achieve my win with grace, and reach the pinnacle of success.

Chapter 8

Choose to Win

"A quitter never wins-and- a winner never quits."
– Napoleon Hill

For much of my life, I did not choose to win. I was going with the flow and praying for more but, when I considered investing in a business opportunity, I was concerned about what my retirement would look like and how I could achieve a better quality of life for myself. I was aware that I had to change something big in my life if I wanted to make things better financially, but I was still uncertain about joining the direct selling industry, or, as it is often called, multi-level marketing. It was all completely new to me, and I had no clue about how to build a business.

Also, there was so much prejudice out there toward the industry and I was not really prepared to overcome the objections being voiced. Now, of course, I know that it is a lack of knowledge and education that makes people think badly about direct selling. They hear general comments casting aspersions, and some people may have had a bad experience, like encountering an unethical person, failing to be successful at direct selling themselves, or being taken in by an outrageous offer they just couldn't resist. And, so, I was hesitant to face what others might think of me for doing this work, and all the scenarios I was hearing about or envisioning told me not to become a direct marketer. I was particularly upset and scared of what my closest family members and friends would think about it.

I now know that, in my experience, those situations I just described are not necessarily representative of the industry. What I have found true is that people choose the company and product that suits their core values. It is better not to base your opinion of the industry on generalizations that have been clouded by the human factor. For me, the company's relationship with the "Napoleon Hill Foundation" provided great insight into the company's fundamental values.

Still, as you can imagine, it took me a while to tell anyone what I had decided to do, especially as I didn't want to get annoyed by naysayers and their objections. I soon became passionate about the business, which took off quickly. It took a great deal of willpower, but it was worth it. And, the industry was nothing like I had been told by outsiders. Far from it. For where I was in my life, I could not have aimed higher. The direct selling industry represents billions and billions of dollars worldwide, and helps hundreds of millions of families overcome poverty and build wealth. I kept my head up and grew my business because I knew that I would find the right people, at the right time, and do it with patience and grace.

How was my experience? What was it like? I began in January 2011, with my flip chart under my arm. I went on, week after week, during snowstorms, spending long days on the road doing meetings and presentations, training, and staying after late evening meetings to learn more. In other words, I did what needed to be done. There was some loneliness, but that's just a challenge every pioneer has to overcome when opening a new marketplace. I also had to face a lot of closed minds, especially in the beginning, and I might have momentarily felt like a thief when a rude objection or epithet was thrown at me. But, I learned to hang on and overcome the objections. Some of the people who first objected saw my great attitude and were able to bear witness to my growth, at which point they suddenly became more interested in the proposition of how I might help them to succeed. More than a few of those people have come back to me and asked questions, re-evaluating their fear-based mentality.

Along the way, I realized that my situation was similar to what I faced as an actress. There, too, I had to accept criticism and the *"nos"* without taking them personally (as per The Second Agreement). I did not let anybody break my dream or my beliefs. I had decided to win! My focus was on one day at a time, one person at a time, one presentation at a time, one client at a time until, one day, I met people who believed hard enough in their own dreams that they decided to win with me; they were committed to their own success!

I had wanted to show my parents and the other people around me that I was building a real business, and I was able to do so. I specifically needed to show my father that I was a winner. One day, he ended up a conversation by asking me, "So, how goes your business?" What he first considered just a funny little something was now a business in his mind. He was taking it seriously. Wow! I had won his pride. And, I ended up being very proud of myself too, recognizing how hard I had worked and knowing that I had proven my commitment in many ways, like missing out on my favourite nighttime TV shows and spending many, many early mornings helping my new partners and their teams.

I reached my first level of leadership after only five months of dedicated, hard team-building work. But, then I hit my first wall and stayed stuck at that rank for two and a half years. What happened? My thinking and my motivation changed while I wasn't looking. I thought, *Well I'm paid pretty well, especially when I compare myself to others who are working more hours than I am but still making about the same amount of money I am.* I wanted to win, and I had won to some degree.

Ultimately, I came to understand why I couldn't reach my very next level. I had won my vision as well! I realized I didn't have another burning desire to fulfill, and that made it harder to push myself past where I was. Plus, my father had acknowledged that I had a business – I was doing something worthwhile and profitable, but that didn't seem like enough of an acknowledgment. I was still holding on to my roots about needing his approval. In short, I needed a "what's next." I am pretty sure you understood from the section on going the extra mile what pulled me out of my blindness. I got myself out of my rut when I achieved my second level of leadership.

Today, I still choose to win and to be free! I tell you all this because it provides a great example of going above and beyond. Also, it is about letting go of generalized misconceptions and learning what is true and not true for yourself.

Find Your Vehicle

"We were created to create, and your ability to dream is paramount and fundamental when it comes to living a dream-come-true life."
– Marcia Wieder

Most people work at a regular, day-to-day job, making money for someone else. Yes, having a steady amount of money coming in gives some people a sense of security but, sometimes, it may not feed their souls. Without a true, authentic purpose, there is no real reward, no sense of self-satisfaction that comes from making a difference in the world. It's sad, but most people don't understand that there is some vehicle outside of their ordinary job that could be more aligned with who they are or would like to become. And, that other thing is what brings a sense of wholeness, which is missing in a lot of people's lives.

I have learned that there is more than one vehicle to which I can bring my passion and my light. I have also found a purpose of equal importance in the writing of this book and the developing of a workshop for others who want to find their light. The behind-the-scenes work I continue to do has shown the universe that I am ready to expand the number of ways I can be of service and help others grow. These opportunities have come to me only now that I am ready to take my place as a helper and teacher of others. And, I still continue my acting career as well.

The rewards for me are many. It is not just about making money. There is great joy in taking on these new roles in life, just as there is joy and fulfillment in being an actress. Regaining the power of my voice and my confidence has taught me how to attract the things I want, and includes a mix of projects that will fulfill me, including public speaking and training. My new vision is not about letting go of what I love, but of attracting opportunities that align with my essence — whether that is continuing to lead my teams, coaching entrepreneurs or running workshops. The satisfaction will come from helping others find their own light and showing them how to make it shine brilliantly.

At the simplest level, my vehicle is my voice and the emotion I willingly share with others. I would not have known that without all the hard work that went into learning how to serve my clients and partners, which is when I was able to realize that I'm at my best when I'm leading people. When I am assisting them, and showing them how not to fall but how to continue to walk and master what they have to learn, I am in the right place, helping others become greater.

Decide and Commit

"If you respect yourself enough to keep commitments even when it's inconvenient to do so, others will come to respect you too."
– Napoleon Hill

As you can see, there are many parts to my vehicle; my voice can express itself in so many ways. I did not discover its true scope all at once, and that is as it should be. We cannot scatter our attention everywhere at the beginning of our journey. At every stage, a new opportunity to learn and grow appears, and it needs to be explored with all your spirit and your heart. The same is true when you first find your vehicle.

There may be many sides to the vehicle you choose but, at some point, you have to decide where to start. You have to commit to things one at a time and, if you open your eyes to the universe, it is likely that you will be shown the right way to proceed. For me, it was all about building up my business first to help lift myself out of poverty. Only then, when I had learned and become skilled at doing things successfully, could I help other people do the same thing. Then, leading a team helped me see that I was, in truth, a leader. My experience choosing some wrong team members, followed by right ones (and not always in this particular order) helped me refine how I seek out and identify people who really want to be helped. Those are the people to whom I can be of service without harming myself emotionally, and I can experience satisfaction from working with them. And, now, I have expanded my vehicle into coaching and writing a book so that I can be of more service.

As with everything, I did not immediately understand what needed to be done. I had to come to the realization that I am someone who has known difficulty and persevered. I had to also understand that I am really committed to accomplishing my goals. I am someone who is accountable. But, I had to see where I was doing all those wonderful things in a way that was not good for me. Being committed to something else at the expense of my health and my faith meant I could not commit to my own value, just to other people. That had to stop. You cannot fully commit to anything unless you commit to yourself first. And, when you commit to a faith in yourself, you can begin to trust your own instincts and move forward through instinctive action.

If you feel that your life is not moving forward, it is likely you are not sufficiently committed. You must make a decision and then act on it. Have you honestly and completely made the decision within your heart? Are you committed to doing what it takes to make that decision a reality? And, are you committed to achieving what you want in an authentic manner, one that is true to who you are as a person? If so, then you will get the results you want when the time is right.

However, it is very easy to lie to ourselves. When that happens, we must go all the way back and look at our vision. We need to ask ourselves, "Is this really right for me?" And, if it is, "Am I committed enough? Am I exchanging some sacrifice in order to get more? Am I in it for the long-term?"

I say all this from experience. When I was attending the workshop that first introduced me to the thought of writing this book, I began to look at the relationship between commitment and result. I went back and re-read Napoleon Hill's chapters on personality and going the extra mile. It reminded me that sometimes we may be committed, but resisting some thing or some part of the process.

When I look at myself, when I acknowledge that I am in one season or another, or being too edgy, I must acknowledge that I choose to win but may not be committed enough to make those little sacrifices that will definitely move me along. For example, perhaps I am reluctant to start a real conversation with someone or don't have a real interest in that person, but cannot advance on my journey until I do so in a heartfelt way. Or, I may be trying to get results by selling for the sake of selling, rather than out of a desire to be of help. For me, being committed and deciding to help people is something that must be done in a genuine way.

Be Authentic

"Sometimes the bravest and most important thing you can do is just show up."
– Brené Brown

When I see myself craving results rather than trusting in the process, it is because there is something that is not aligned with my true intent and my authentic self. This is true for the people I coach as well. When they are struggling, it is often because they are not being authentic. When that happens, I often have to show them some tough love, without saying things in a rough way. (Sometimes, being authentic means being honest with someone; you cannot help them if you cannot show them their truth.) I suggest they really look inside and decide if they are envisioning the right thing for themselves. Or, are they being too hard on themselves by demanding an immediate result? Are they comparing their results to those of someone else with either much more experience or who is acting out in an inauthentic way?

I do the same thing for myself, remembering that it is all about walking the talk as well as the walk. I am the one to decide if I will win, and with what intent I will win. And, when I say I will win, I do. But, I do not always get to decide the timing of that win. Sometimes, the universe controls the situation, and it tells me when my commitment is not in alignment with my integrity. You cannot achieve something when you are not following all the rules that you committed to follow when you made your agreements to yourself.

Sometimes being authentic hurts because it means showing a vulnerable side of who we are deep inside. I am authentic in a very loving, committed way of being true to what I think. I say it like it is, and that is especially important when coaching someone who is lying to themself. Being authentic can take a lot of courage, but it gives as much as it takes. Being authentic has given me the courage to talk about the need behind the pain, and to work with people who may initially intimidate me with their greatness. Being authentic is talking about truth and being aligned with your own value.

Do Whatever It Takes

"Don't stop when you are tired. Stop when you are done."
– Unknown

This is an extremely powerful statement, but it must not be taken the wrong way. It is not about pushing others aside, or ruthlessly getting to the top. Doing whatever it takes means learning what you need to learn, being committed in your actions and choosing to ask for support. The objective is to become an enlightened warrior who can lead you into battle and be victorious.

You need to be focused on and aligned with the action that will take you to the next level. It can involve attending seminars and workshops, working with a coach, reading books or availing yourself of other support that will bring you to the point where you can take that next step. Some of this may involve investing money, but doing what it takes is definitely not only about things that cost you to go to the next level. It also involves taking a look at your own personality and honestly assessing what needs to be corrected in order to continue on your journey. There will be healing, forgiving yourself for past actions that caused you to hurt yourself, and meditating. It's a matter of humility and, although this may be a hard step for you to take, it is essential. Keep in mind that your intent is not to tear yourself down, but to build yourself up to your innate greatness.

Doing what it takes must be associated with hope and moving ahead. It means making the choice to strive for more rather than settle for your regular life, and to come out of your comfort zone because you have the desire to learn, listen, find your balance, and respect yourself. If you are not happy where you are, then you need to acknowledge that you deserve to be happy and become fully committed to doing what it takes to get there. It may take you time, and that is okay. I needed more than a season of reflection, seminars and the writing of this book to bring myself to my new level of commitment, and I am infinitely better and happier for it.

Move On

"When the going is hardest, just keep on keeping on, and you'll get there sooner than someone who finds the going easy."
– Napoleon Hill

Sometimes in life we can become paralyzed, held in place by our roots. Other times, we may have the sense of not moving at all, but that's only because our outward actions are on hold while we are healing our inner wounds and processing new information. For me, those moments are often followed by a sudden shift in consciousness, similar to the one I had recently. It is almost like someone flipped a switch and turned on a light. We are transformed in some way, and then we can move on. But, it is important to recognize that, even when we think we are standing still, we are not. What goes on behind-the-scenes is critical movement forward, even if it doesn't always seem so.

In the larger sense, move on means getting out of our own way and contributing to the lives of others. When we turn our attention to being of service, we get a greater sense of well-being and gain a healthy pride that will sustain us during the hard work to follow. Many of the chapters in this book talk about this definition of moving on because it is so critical to improving our lives.

Stick to It

"Do not let anything that happens in life be important enough that you're willing to close your heart over it."
– Michael A. Singer

When things are not going your way, or when you think your progress is too slow, you can be tempted to quit. But, that is absolutely the last thing you should do. Commitment means staying in the game. Nothing will be easy all the time. There will be seasons, and an ebb and flow to your progress that you cannot lose hope over. Instead, it is at those times you must commit, and decide every day to be authentic. See where you are out of balance or not in alignment with your integrity, and continue to do whatever it takes to move on and shift.

Perseverance triumphs. Having my own home, the house I wrote about earlier, is a major win in my life, and it would not have been possible if I had not stuck with what I am doing. There have been times in the six plus years I have been building my business that were not good for me, but I did not give up, nor did I turn my back on this wonderful opportunity.

There is a big difference, however, between being stubborn and being persistent. The former implies that you just won't move and the other means never give up, keep at it. When I was younger, my parents would sometimes tell me that I was being stubborn or closed-minded. The thing is, I wasn't. I was being persistent, continuing to press my point to win an issue. The thing is, if I hadn't been that way I would not have achieved so many goals. I stick to it, learning, growing, doing whatever it takes until I get what I want. And, it doesn't matter how long it takes.

Let me give you an example of what I'm talking about when I say keep at it, no matter what. My first three years resulted in an income that was astonishing to me. I was amazed by the way I was attracting abundance and how that led to my being able to buy my house. I was so grateful and happy to give back and be of service. The problem is that I became so focused on helping my downline teams that I forgot about building new partnerships of my own. In other words, I was doing good things and being of service, but – yet again – I was focusing too much on bettering others without protecting or building my own success. And, I was not appreciated for all I was doing for my teams.

Much the same is true about my career as an actress. There too, I put so much time and emotion into being an administrator of one type or another for my profession, and protecting the rights and conditions of other actors, that I had little strength or focus to build my own career.

In putting the needs of the many in front of my own, I was part of my own undoing, hurting relationships that might have been beneficial to me.

I had to look at why I was attracting people who disrespected me and expected me to do the work for them. Ultimately, I realized that I needed to lead without carrying others on my shoulders. I had to teach and then let them fall as I had fallen. Only then could they develop the ability to fully commit to something and stick with it.

I also had to grasp that I needed a better sense of who to choose for my team, who was ready to be led and nurtured and who could form true partnerships with me that were beneficial to both of us. That is what my business is all about. Now, because I have done so much work loosening the roots that made me think I did not deserve success, I find myself more aligned with the respect that I deserve. The people who are attracted to me now that I have done my inner work are those who are ready to spread their wings and contribute to the lifestyles of others. That's who I am looking for, and many more will continue to come to me.

Plus, I will be a better coach to the people that come because I am able to assist them right where they are at the moment. And, I am able to do so without falling into the need of being acknowledged and loved. I now have the strength to put limits on what I do for others and, in its own way, that is better for them as well as it means they must choose to win and examine what may be holding them back from achieving the results they envision. My intent is contributing to their growth in a meaningful way that is also healthy for me.

The point of telling you all this is that having come to these realizations allows me to stick with my business which is still an important vehicle. I will continue to learn from what did not go well in the past and build upon that learning. I will also continue to recover from the hurt and rejection I am going through, as well as the unhappiness I endured from renting out my house to someone who was not respectful. At the same time, I will continue to expand my voice further into coaching and teaching. You must start in one area, but you can stick with many facets of your true vehicle. Doing so is what will give me my greatest satisfaction and success.

Now, when people see me again and again, they see a woman that walks the talk and is going to achieve what she wants by sticking with it and doing what needs to be done. Everyone can become one of those people that others refer to as a person who walks the talk. Everyone can be a success, achieve their vision, and have a fulfilling and rewarding life. My question is: Are you on your way to doing that or will you go beyond for a greater purpose?

Chapter 9

Live Your Mission

*"Outstanding people have one thing in common:
an absolute sense of mission."*
– Zig Ziglar

Every time I immerse myself in a new workshop or open my mind to accepting new information about myself, I take a giant step ahead. This is why I stressed the importance of continuous learning in an earlier chapter. A recent series of seminars has opened my eyes to something transformative that has already begun to make a difference in my life.

I have known for a quite a while that having a vision is essential to creating success, but now I see how critical it is also to have a mission. It is important to understand the fundamental difference between these two words; namely that one leads us into action while the other is our contribution to the world. A mission gives you purpose. It is a meaning for your life that comes from your inner self, and it motivates you to action. Your vision is part of your outer world, and it is what leads to attaining money.

As a gifted actress, who did not believe in my own talent, I could not sufficiently enlighten myself and, as such, could not create a vision that would steer me toward superior parts that I wanted to play. However, when I discovered through my company how to have a vision and how to concretize the principles of Napoleon Hill, I discovered that my inner self work was what I needed to do before I could bring my vision to life. And, that realization led me to my mission, which is to enlighten myself first, master my life, express myself authentically, create with passion, and then inspire others to do the same by connecting with them at a higher level.

How amazing it was to discover that the more I was working on myself, and the more I was humbled through the learning process, the better I was as a teacher helping people to succeed. This new understanding of my life's purpose crystallized during discovery exercises at a New Peaks transformational program. I came to see that everything has always been about how I may serve others better because I was, by default, trying to do that all along. But, I was often hurting myself while trying to help others, and that was not the universe's intention.

Enlightenment came when I realized why I had to take a step back each time I faced something in my own mirror. I used to agonize over what I perceived as "stops" along the way, but these moments of reflection and learning were part of fulfilling my mission. I was moving ahead although I did not realize it at the time. I have been walking this dual path of self-healing and reaching out to help others for many years. Although I only recently defined my mission, I have owned it for a long time. The difference is that today, I am no longer afraid of others and, as a result, I can give back from a place of self-confidence. I can tap into my greatness and my ability to empathize without giving so much of myself that I sabotage my own life along the way. I have become a better communicator, and I speak from a place of hope rather than react to old hurts. What a cycle of change!

You are likely to find that you, too, have owned your life's mission without totally understanding it or putting it to use in a way that brings you happiness, joy, and prosperity. If you look inside for inspiration and take stock of your personality, assets, and skills, you can live your mission and make your vision reality.

Live Your Mission

Find Your Niche

"You gotta keep trying to find your niche and trying to fit into whatever slot that's left for you to make one of your own."
– Dolly Parton

What are your natural talents? What skills do you most enjoy using? What activities give you the most satisfaction, emotionally, physically, and spiritually? These characteristics will help you find the area in which you can honour those gifts, find satisfaction, make money, and do good for others. Think of it as your calling. Are you meant to do and create, or help others to do those things? Are you a practical person who can manage to organize and get things done when others can't? Or, are you a great listener, who can hear the hidden text in someone else's words? Each of these talents will lead you down a different path.

If the thought of identifying where you belong in the world sounds a bit overwhelming, do not worry. When you are ready, the universe will show you your niche. Before I started to build my business, I had no intention of working in direct selling. It wasn't even a thought in my mind. In fact, when I first received samples of the coffee I had a bad reaction to the concept because of the way it was sold. In truth, I did not understand that why it was different and more aligned with my principles. At the same time, my focus was solely on being a powerful, working actress. I was not looking to do anything else, even though I was a bit desperate financially.

When Michel Desjardins, my sponsor, gave me samples and saw my reaction to the concept of direct selling, he explained that the company was associated with the "Napoleon Hill Foundation" and that it practiced the principles of helping and teaching, embodying a partnership between company and staff that was historical. Then, my friend asked if I had ever read "Think and Grow Rich." Of course, at that point, I didn't even know who Napoleon Hill was. Now, when I speak to people about him, I tell them he is the grandfather of "The Secret," which is an easier reference for younger generations. I also tell them about how he has inspired generations to create their philosophy through the reading of his books.

The book opened my eyes — 25,000 of the people he had interviewed were failures, and only 500 were successful. Then, for me to learn that what separated the successful people from the failures was a common ability to be spiritually, financially, personally, and professionally aligned – well, it was a revelation. People had become millionaires because of that book!

In many ways, I had no choice but to learn the system. I knew that I needed to find something worth working at. I had to change, and this was the opportunity to do so. It was also the first time I decided to let myself be helped by someone else. After all, I had no clue about being an entrepreneur. I didn't know what was involved. And, I was scared. So, I knew I had to let go of expecting myself to know everything on my own. I could not worry about being a perfectionist. I had to accept that there was going to be a learning curve and that others knew more than I did so I had to be open to learning from them.

My business was clearly in the right niche for me at the time. Little by little, in five months, I was able to detach myself from the results and really become of service, something which I was not in acting because I could not let go of the frustration that came from not being hired for months at a time. I discovered the rules and principles that were right for me. There was a process to follow. I saw that there are things that repulse and others that attract. And so, I thought, *I will study that.*

This timing was also aligned with my true path as the company was introduced to the Quebec market and, so, I was able to be a pioneer and to step out of my comfort zone. This has put me in a position to experience some of the success I never expected. And, now, my learning and growth is helping build my niche which, in turn, will help me be of greater service to more people.

Be of Service

"Every day use your magic to be of service to others."
– Marcia Wieder

The principles of Napoleon Hill have shown me that being of service is essential. As it says in "Think and Grow Rich," *"It is literally true that you can succeed best and quickest by helping others to succeed."* As I learned through my own experience, this does not mean doing the work for someone else, but rather guiding and teaching them how to gain success on their own.

Helping others starts with imparting what I've learned from my own experience and the many seminars and workshops I've attended over the years. I can share business tools and practices with others as well, but the most important thing I can do is help people understand and overcome those things that are holding them back. Most often, business problems are not really about business – at least not just about the surface business issues. Rather, those problems are intertwined with relationship and behavioural failings that grow down to the roots. Some business coaches can assist with the practical issues and teach someone to manage their time better, but most are not skilled at helping someone reach deep down inside themselves and confront what is really holding them back.

Working and sharing with like-minded people and the wonderful mentors I've had has helped me understand the theory behind difficult behaviours — both in myself and other people. I am now able to assist others in finding the roots of their discontent and unproductive behaviours, and then guide them in tugging at those roots and changing how they interact with the world. This is a gift that I have been given and I have studied and practiced how to do it well. After going through the horrible things I have gone through, and having done years of work on myself, I can now access a complete range of techniques for helping others who are experiencing difficulties in their relationships or challenges in life.

How To Ignite Your Inner Strength

Create Your Tools

"The quality of your life is equal to the quality of your rituals."
– Adam Markel

I have developed my own daily habits as rituals and have powerful tools that help me stay connected with my greater purpose at a higher level. This allows me to stay in a calm and positive frame of mind so that I can maintain a better, healthier support to my way of listening, acting and responding appropriately. Too many people fall back into a negative frame of mind if there is bad news on the TV or someone criticizes them even a little bit. We can't move ahead that way. Reverting to the negative happens unconsciously, but we can keep ourselves centred and right-thinking by employing strategies and taking actions that keep us positive.

My daily activities keep me centred. Mine is a personalized ritual to actualize goals and achieve better outcomes in my interactions with other people (as well as financially). These tools and rituals also help me generate more focus and success. Create your own tools for nurturing and nourishing your soul, body, and heart. Find the things that make you happy and build them into your plans for the day.

That may mean giving yourself a little bit more time to de-stress, perhaps by taking a walk, playing with a pet or spending more meaningful time with friends. Laughing is a wonderful tool. Find out what it is that brings you laughter and joy so you can continue taking care of all the parts of who you are and make space for your inner child to play. Meditation helps centre yourself, as it brings your spirit forth in order to be nourished and helps you be at peace in a quiet zone. And, no, you don't need to sit and hum AOHMMMMMMMM for hours at a time (ha, ha, ha).

I take some time to journal (I've been journaling since I was a youth) and have been shown more deeply, working with Marcia, how I can interact with the different parts of myself. This may bring you more acceptance of your true self without any pressure. Taking stock of your emotions and acknowledging them can help you let the negative ones go. I have also found it essential to work with a mentor, and I do that at least once a month.

When I coach people, I bring them all kinds of precious tools to help them handle their reactions and behaviours in specific situations. It can be as easy as bringing awareness to the present moment, breathing before you speak when addressing something difficult, or bringing yourself peace by using and remembering a piece of spiritual writing that calms you. Yes, these are inward-based tools, but they have a profound effect on your outside actions. It is important to remember that you are looking to build good relationships, and that includes the one with yourself. Or, should I say yourselves? By that I mean, for me, there is my inner child, the business woman, the daughter and sister, and the artist! (hum, hum…and the lover is coming, ha, ha, ha.)

Another critical tool is the one of letting go. "The Dark Side of the Light Chasers" by Debbie Ford had a huge impact on me in working with Marcia, especially when she conducted our "Shadow Initiation." Our shadow work has given me an opportunity to study the book, and doing the exercises in it gave me, as my ultimate tool, the knowledge and ability to embrace my shadow. This book is renowned for helping you reclaim and heal your lost parts as you discover how to better accept your wholeness.

All of these tools are meant to help me design what better suits me so I can reach a point of manifesting my personal essence. They can do the same for you! Fight for yourself and reach something or someone to whom you can deliver help and, by doing so, develop your own sense of serenity.

Utilize Your Gift

"Your talent is God's gift to you.
What you do with it is your gift back to God."
– Leo Buscaglia

My gift is to help others transcend the behaviours and feelings that keep them from being successful, both personally and professionally. I share what I have been taught, and teach them how to do the same things for themselves. More than that, I have been given such beautiful tools so I can show others how to discover their own gifts. Many people believe that they are not gifted, but all of us excel at something that can make the world better. Usually, you are already doing something by default, so you take it for granted. Your gift may seem simple, but that doesn't make it less of a gift. Any benevolent action is a gift. You may be compassionate, listen well, or be especially patient. Being creative, that is being able to write, paint or make music, means having a gift that fulfills you and enriches others. And, since so much of the world is not yet on enough of a spiritual path, the thing you do is needed. It is so easy to forget how important such things are because we are so oriented to completing tasks and focusing on results. We often forget how valuable these gifts that are connected to the heart and the soul are.

Use your gifts, if not in your current professional life, then as something that brings joy to you and others. You will almost always see how to build your life around that gift, and that doing so will bring you what you most want in life. It is also true that many of us find a way to generate income using our gifts.

This winter I was in total burnout. I had been constantly running and doing for the last six years, almost without stopping to take a single breath, and my soul was beaten up. Recovering from such an exhausting period of stress has given me the chance to concentrate on the activities that bring me peace, which I desperately needed after my overambitious doing had overwhelmed me. I began to create new rituals as well, and that allowed me to draw, play, and finish my book. In doing these activities, I was being as benevolent as I could be to myself. During this transitional period, I used all the gifts I have for my book and the "Human Circles of Life" workshop I was developing at the time.

Live Your Mission

Brand Yourself

"Your Brand is what people say about you when you leave the room."
– Jeff Bezos

Being exceptional at something isn't enough on its own. It's important that others know you are an expert, someone who can help them, and that they are attracted to you. To do that, you need to create a Brand. My co-author, Raymond Aaron, an authority on branding for small businesses, refers to it as your Brand, with a capital "B." It is amazing to be taken under his wing as he is so enlightened, both personally and professionally. In my mind, Raymond is a great mentor and teacher. It was from him and from the "Guerrilla Business School" that I learned why branding is so important, and how it can build your business. Other people need to know who you are, what you do, and why you do it better or differently than anyone else. Branding does that. Done properly, it also gets you known and respected. The most important thing about your Brand is that others define it, and they are the people who know you and have worked with you. It is their perception of your worth, and it defines why clients and partners should want to do business with you.

Many Diamond level colleagues see me as a leader but, in truth, I am still discovering my Brand. I do know that at least a big part of it has to do with being fun to work with, even when we go deep. I didn't decide this on my own. It happened during an event at which I was privileged to present the Mission Message part of the presentation. A huge delegation of Leadership had come to Montreal (this was a big deal) to energize and enthuse us by telling their success stories.

During his speech, an Elite Black Diamond branded me the "Chief Fun Officer" (CFO). Then, another Diamond, spoke about why people follow leaders. During his speech, he used me as an example and said I attract people because I'm contagious. I was blown away! Since that day, because of my energy level and the way I love to laugh, I am the contagious CFO.

It's a great Brand, and it reflects a wonderful gift – to make people happy. I am known for my sense of humour, my ability to create joy, and the impact I have when I speak.

When I think about it, this is not as surprising as you might believe. I present myself as I am.. I have not told my story before this book, which represents a kind of coming out of the closet for me. It is scary in many ways, but I know that telling my story, talking about the things that happened and sharing my way of overcoming them with courage and resilience will help so many people. Think of how amazing it is to come out of that and be seen as the CFO.

Will this be my Brand as a mentor and teacher? I do not yet know, just as you will not know what your Brand is until other people tell you. Then, if it is a good Brand, you will need to live up to it. That gives you something to strive for and something that you can feel good about. For me, being Branded is being uplifted and associated with something worthwhile and helpful to others. If being a provider of fun is my higher-level promise, I am happy with that.

Spread It to the World

"The Meaning of Life is to Find Your Gift. The Purpose Is to Give It Away."
– Pablo Picasso

A gift must be shared. Just as I am compelled to take what I have learned and teach others how to have a happier and more successful life, you will want people to know about what you can do to make their lives better. Your mission is aligned with your inner world, but taking your message to the outer world is an important part of your journey. When I am on stage or working with motivated team members, I am fulfilling my purpose. I am alive and fulfilled. My life has meaning, and it is by focusing on sharing my gifts that I best put aside those things in my life that might otherwise drag me down.

The more people I can help, the better my life will be. That is our higher purpose and, as Napoleon Hill and many other amazing mentors have said, it is by making the world better that we are a success. The Law of

Live Your Mission

Attraction says we must open ourselves up and ask the universe for what we want. We must see the joys of life coming true for them actually to come true. And, that happens when we share our hearts and souls with others. When we lift them up, we lift ourselves up too.

If my business partners take our work together seriously, then I want this opportunity — whichever one it is — to be their chance at a better life, one with more freedom, more joy, and more juice. Because, really, the only thing that matters to me is to understand and help human beings, especially those with whom I do business. I do what I do for them; they are the future of my success. But, they have to embrace their challenges as completely as I do.

Chapter 10

The Real Connection

"Faith is the spiritual 'chemical' which, when it is mixed with prayer, gives one direct and immediate connection with Infinite Intelligence."
– *Napoleon Hill*

We are so much more than just our physical being and the things and people that surround us. For me, I must connect to both my soul and a higher power within me to be at peace. It is a bit hard to talk about this subject as no one has the same definition of what is bigger than we humans, but keep in mind that it has nothing to do with religion. It is whatever you call it for your own self. I call it my higher self. I'm talking about having a spiritual connection to both yourself and to something greater or higher than yourself. My truth is that healing my inner self, connecting with my soul, and acknowledging a higher power nurture me more than anything else. I read and listen to great spiritual teachers such as Eckhart Tolle, Greg Braden, and Lee Carroll, and their words reconnect me with meaning.

"The Meaning Institute," with Marcia and the community she creates for us, was the perfect program for reconnecting my heart and soul at a deeper level. Believe it or not, I am grateful for all parts of my journey, even if that may sound incomprehensible to you. I connect with other people who have this openness. Some may think, *Dominique, your story is not one of peace; all told, it was somewhat of a nightmare.* Of course, there have been many bad things and horrible moments in my life, but my passion fuels my quest. I can't put into words how I feel, but being a seeker of meaning and truth is my greatest privilege. The ultimate experience is finding peace even when nothing makes sense. Once we come to a philosophical point of serenity, there is always something bigger, and it is the support of our friends to help us overcome whatever it is we are facing, or achieve a breakthrough that brings relief.

I have been on the road to spirituality since I was a teen and I am grateful to share this part of my path with you. I want to help you feel what it is like to live in the middle of both dark and light when experiencing your life path. As with many of my steps forward, I was in a five-day camp called "Wizard." Being led with significance is priceless. I learned about surrendering to the universe and seeing it in between things as they are (or seem to be). When I am acting from my heart, and being driven by something that is bigger than me, I understand that everything is helpful and in the right place. We know from inside ourselves that difficult situations, delays, and disappointments are all part of the universe's plan and they are happening for a reason – usually so that we can learn a lesson and grow as a human being.

It is only when I came to love myself that I could connect with the universe in a truly positive way. For me, this connection leads to a higher state of consciousness. I call it the love connection as it combines loving yourself, loving your life, and loving others (or at least treating them in a respectful way). Having faith and following our heart lets us express our essence in a powerful way. It releases positive energy and the Law of Attraction in ways I can't always see in the moment.

This spiritual connection, to me, is so powerful that it often brings me to tears. I have been given wisdom and a magical way to receive serenity. The universe provides because I am connected. I put out positivity and peace and I receive those things in return.

When do you feel connected to your soul? Do you have something in your life that gives you faith, a faith that all is happening as it should? And, when you don't feel connected spiritually, what do you do to come to that place of inner peace? Is there a book or an audio that helps you get your spirit, body, soul, and heart in total alignment?

I know that I am an old soul and that there's more than we know about who we truly are. I lost my sense of self-worth along the way and believed I had to fight, but this is what it means to experience humanity. I am more passionate about this real connection than I am about keeping my old mindfulness about what society wants us to believe.

Perhaps you can find a special place or ritual that helps you develop this sense of something greater. A space all your own gives you the time to align yourself with love from within and without. That will help you achieve a sense of serenity and honour your body as you would a temple. Spirituality and serenity are gifts we experience as we beautify our souls on our journey here on earth.

LOVE, the Acronym*

I have developed my own acronym to easily remind myself how better everything is when we embody love. I created acronyms a lot when I was young, making cards and writing poems for the people closest to me. I created this one for this book. The acronym also makes a great creative tool. It is my MOTTO and reminds me how important it is to love. I hope it will keep my CFO-spirit with you as you go forward on your path. Loving ourselves and treating others with love is not only powerful, but needed. I carry this acronym with me to nurture my bliss.

Light Up Your Soul
Overcome Fears
Visualize Your Virtues
Empower

*Free bonus to be obtained on www.IgniteYourInnerStrengthCoach.com

Follow Your Heart

"Your vision will become clear only when you can look into your own heart. Who looks outside, dreams; who looks inside, awakes."
– Carl Jung

The heart cannot lie to you. Sometimes we choose not to hear it or we listen to it but then ignore what it says. I have gone through life largely following my heart, and it was at those moments that I experienced almost all of my happiness and freedom. At other times, I should have made my heart my navigation system, my GPS, but my rational head pushed ahead and sent me far off course.

There is a congruence between the heart and the soul. Your heart says yes or no. You can tap into that feeling, and know that you are moving in the right direction. When you find yourself debating, studying the pros and cons of a decision, that is your head taking charge. Sometimes the rational decision is not the best choice for each of us as an individual. It is difficult to motivate yourself or go the distance when your "heart's just not in it." A decision from the heart drives you into action, but a choice made solely in your head invites inertia or leaves you "all over the place" or in procrastination mode.

Your heart is your connection to your spiritual self. It is what lifts you up. There is something so powerful, deep inside you, and that brings you to a totally different level. When your heart is at its fullest, you are truly alive and you have a depth of feeling that cannot be vanquished. I am always "from the bottom of my heart," throwing myself all in to help people reach their fullest heart. What makes you feel alive? What empowers you through passion? Do you make your decisions based on what your heart says or do you bow to the head and live a life that is not all it can be? In other words, does your heart beat for you or against you?

If you are a very practical person, you may not think about this amazing connection between heart and soul, but I can assure you that, when you are in the middle of that connection, you will feel it. There will be no doubt. You may experience a sense of detachment from what is happening around you; enjoy it. Revel in it. Clarity will follow. The heart needs care. It must be taught to love on many levels. How do you handle your heart? Do you treat it well, and with respect? Or, do you allow it to be broken?

.

The Real Connection

My Body, My Temple

"The body is your temple. Keep it pure and clean for the soul to reside in."
–*B.K.S. Iyengar*

The emotional and spiritual aspects of our lives are critical, but so is our relationship with the physical. When we don't learn the lessons of life, and when we don't take care of ourselves, we feel it in our body. When we ignore our bodies, we are not connected to the present nor are we listening to what the body has to say. We don't understand that the aches and pains are warning signs, messages from our heart that we need to take better care of ourselves. So, we don't give ourselves the time to recuperate from an illness or even over-exertion. We may totally forget to nurture the body properly. Illness thrives when the link between your spirit and your body is broken. Emotions are magnified and it is much easier to over-react and misinterpret circumstances and conversations.

When I was younger, I was in very good shape. I played tennis, danced, and did gymnastics. I knew that having a good body and being agile were important to my acting. Even when I was taking drugs, my good metabolism kept me looking fit, but I was certainly not taking care of my body. And, then, when I was going through everything two years ago, I became less physically active. My depression contributed to this, of course, but it was more than that. I had taken my physical abilities for granted and did not honour or maintain them. Ultimately, not taking care of my body caught up with me and I began to injure myself and suffer from aches and pains.

So, I ask you to consider the following questions:

- Are you in touch with your body?
- Are you feeling aches and pains? What do you do about them?
- Do you treat your body like a temple?
- Do you do too much and exhaust yourself on a regular basis?
- Do you exercise regularly? And, when you train, is it because you want to be fit and look great or do you want to be healthy? (Over-

training to look good on the outside is not healthy; it is not taking care of your body.)

When I used drugs, I created a persona: the funny Rock 'n Roll gal that made everyone laugh. I was on a search to feel (or not feel) things, but these patterns of pain and pleasure were taken to excess and still didn't fill my inner emptiness. I loved to party. I was edgy and looking for fun so that my friends would like me. I wanted them to be fascinated by my joy and ways of entertaining them all. But, as soon as I was back home, I would cry for my life. That's when I wrote myself a letter in which I was clear about why I was sabotaging myself. My greatest fear was that we are powerful beyond measure. That's why I began my book with the amazing poem "Our Greatest Fear" by Marianne Williamson.

When I stopped taking drugs, I was caught in a laziness that I couldn't bear, seeing myself lose such precious time. At the time, I was completely disconnected from my heart, body and soul. I had never done drugs on my job or on the stage, but I was yearning to transform my relationship with my wholeness. I had to stop needing to numb my feelings as that only kept me in confusion longer. I looked up the location of a Narcotics Anonymous (NA) meeting. I'll say this straight, just the way I spoke at the time. I brought my ass and put it on a chair; I was longing to share and state that yes, I was dependent on drugs, that I was suffering and that I needed help. I stayed with the NA meetings for quite a few years, long enough to stay on track, but my multiple dependency issues made me a target for men. Some members were actually helpful but, again, my lack of discernment brought me into two different "sad adventures" that resulted in my becoming pregnant (twice in a six-month period). I decided to look for another kind of therapy and reached out for another kind of support for myself.

During a hypnosis session, the man conducting the session explained to me how taking drugs had brought me to the "unconscious collectivity" side and how this was contributing to my paranoia and magnifying all my attitudes and rejections of self.

Chapter 11

Being Mentored

"Mentors are people who have wisdom,
resources or skills that can help you pivot."
– Adam Markel

Many people have come into my life at one time or another and taught me, either through example or something they said. Many times, these people become an important part of my life, if even only for a short time. In other instances, the lesson came from a speaker I heard once or the author of a book that particularly resonated with me.

I don't believe that I found all of these incredible people on my own. The universe had a hand in bringing me to different lecturers, authors and teachers, each offering a different kind of help. And, having studied and worked with many trainers and mentors over these last years, I have developed a good intuition for who is walking their talk and operating from a place of love and support.

In the last six years, I have been mentored by so many men and women who have given me the real definition of a mentor. The leaders of my company have influenced my life tremendously, especially when I attended conventions or had the opportunity to be the student of a Master Teacher in the seminars and programs I have taken.

It's a privilege to share the sum of my learning with you in this chapter. But, first, I want to tell you about how I discovered my mentors and ended up following them; also, how at some level I became one too.

Not everyone who calls themselves a mentor is one, and not every so-called "guru" is worth your time or money. However, I know from my own experience that having great mentors changes everything. I continue to learn something profound at almost every one of the workshops in which I participate. I have also been honoured to interact one-on-one with people who are further along on their own path than I am on mine, and the experiences have been mind and heart altering.

In this chapter, I want to talk about what makes someone a great mentor, and tell you about those individuals that have had the greatest effect on me. These mentors have inspired and influenced me over time, and continue to do so to this day.

The Meaning of MENTOR*

Just as I use the acronym "LOVE," I also made the word mentor into an acronym that represents my definition of what a great mentor is and does. It also summarizes what I want to share with you in this chapter.

Mindset
Empower
Nurture
Teach
Own Greatness
Raise the Bar

What makes mentors different from the rest of us? Although they go through challenges and seasons of their own, they really manage those circumstances differently. Great mentors are able to master their cycles and difficult situations more quickly than we can. They have developed and cultivated a real universal connection to the Law of Attraction, and behave as though all things are possible.

You cannot find and follow true mentors unless you can see people for who they truly are. Recognizing who has something real to offer is the key to choosing the right mentor for you. Look for mentors who:

- Have a vision
- Master their thoughts
- Believe and have faith
- Have levels of huge competency

- Continue to read and study
- Stay aware of their behaviours and keep them as a level of high standard
- Know how to clean their own personal challenges
- Seek for meaning and inspire people to dig deeper
- Create a difference in other people's lives
- Embody their leadership with strength and courage
- Have the desire to help others to transform their life
- Help people to release what no longer serves them
- Motivate and inspire
- Live by their teachings
- Command respect
- Make their living a continual evolving process
- Overcome their challenges with fierceness
- Walk with confidence
- Master speech
- Continue to grow
- Surround themselves with masterminds, and like-minded and successful people
- Follow the principles of success by putting them into action
- Have a high level of commitment and integrity as part of their daily habits
- Get results and keep aiming higher
- Provide rituals for healing from within

Raise the Bar*

Sometimes, I know that I'm not at a place I need to be, and I work to change that. I'm continuously seeking to improve myself and to become ready for the next step and level of success. This is what I mean when I say I'm always raising the bar for myself. Of course, I am human and so are mentors.

I'd like to take a moment to tell you about a strong woman who inspired me. I have been blessed to learn from her wisdom several years in a row, just before she started a new workshop to foster female empowerment in business and to encourage women to be colleagues more than competitors. Her message is very clear: in business, women need to be more supportive of each other and have a stronger feeling of fellowship, just as men do. She is an inspiration to me, as well as a woman who walks the talk.

I was extremely grateful to have been able to attend her "workshop," which was held the day after our huge "Diamond Weekend" event for several years. At one of her workshops, she talked to us about a women's world and a better way to raise the bar. She also explained how to behave during a tough moment; that really helped me on something and she doesn't even know it.

Here is something I found on Facebook that has been of great help as I continue to walk my walk:

"When things aren't what we'd like them to be in our relationships, our natural tendency is to cast blame externally verses internally. But the truth is that blame breeds weakness and keeps us in bondage! Taking personal responsibility for your happiness and owning your part in the conflict is the only road that leads to peace and happiness in life. I have made friends, lost friends, and vowed to never befriend again. I finally realized that I have the power to edit the script I wrote, produced and directed in my life. So if I don't like the role I'm playing in friendship, I can always write a new script! Thus, this is the RECENT promise I made to ALL of my friends:

1. *I will NEVER do or say anything with the intent to harm, embarrass or betray your trust. I will never allow anyone else to harm, embarrass or betray you. I will NEVER put my personal agenda before what is in your best interest. I will always have your back. <LOYALTY>*
2. *I will always be genuine and truthful about who I am publicly and privately. I will always be myself with you. <AUTHENTICITY>*
3. *When I have an issue with you, I will come to you and only you. I will not discuss you in your absence. My yes is my yes and my no is my no. I will always tell you the truth, good or bad. <HONESTY>*
4. *I will be your encourager and will always give you the benefit of the doubt.I will make it a priority to see your heart. <TRUST>*
5. *I will speak to you kindly and with consideration. I will show support for your choices. I love you...therefore, I love who you love. <RESPECT>*

Please understand that the more you give to the wrong person, the more they resent you because you take away their right to judge you or to be jealous of you. That is why friendship is reserved for only those people in your life who are loyal, honest, authentic, respectful, appreciative and encouraging. Evaluate your current relationships and make the necessary adjustments...you'll be much happier when it is all said and done! This is a lesson I learned the hard way!!!"

–E.B.

*Free bonus to be obtained on www.IgniteYourInnerStrengthCoach.com

My Mentors and Teachers

I want to share some of the values I look for when searching for inspiration, as well as the wisdom and strength of people that attracted me to them. I have gratitude for each of them. Talking about them here is also my way of acknowledging the impact they have had on my way of thinking and growing.

My First Inspirations in Life

Not everyone who teaches you will call themselves a "mentor." Great teachers can come from anywhere. You may not even know that they are being a mentor until well after the fact.

My very first mentor was my father's sister, Aunt Francine. When I was a teenager, she shared with me some of the authors and books that had inspired her. She let me know that I was worthy, and told me about the good and great that was inside me (my sensitivity, my gifts, and my innate talent to express who I was as a young woman). My aunt was among the most powerful sources of support in my struggles. She gave me a copy of the beautiful book by Thomas Moore, "Care of the Soul." Not only did this book open my eyes to the concept of a spiritual world but, to this day, it is a resource I go back to time and time again. My aunt was completely non-judgmental and, when I became an adult, she helped me see that I was a seeker of truth. I could speak with her about things that no one else understood.

Then there was Nicole Rivet, who was a pioneer in her field. Nicole was the Registrar at HEC, an academic administration university. She was in charge of more than sixty employees and responsible for all the student-related operations within her department. I worked for Nicole for a few summers as a receptionist. Her leadership and human core values were challenging for some people because she had a direct way of handling her place in a man's world. I was more attracted by her strength than I was afraid of her commands.

Once, Nicole invited me into her office to get my personal opinion about an employee, and I felt honoured that she considered me to be a truthful person. She saw my bad habits and defense mechanisms and made me confront them more than once. I came in late and was she sometimes caught me in the cafeteria. When this happened, I would make a joke of it, saying that I had come in on time but on "boss time" (ha, ha, ha). It would then turn into a funny conversation, in which she would ask me if she needed to buy me an alarm clock.

Nicole never lost her temper, and I considered her to be a great role model. I observed and admired her. At one point, she encouraged me to pursue my passion and not work just to make money. Specifically, Nicole basically pushed me out the door saying, *"I don't want to see you next summer"* because she wanted me to do what I was meant to do. It is because of Nicole's huge support that I took the leap from amateur to professional actress and prepared my audition to go to The Conservatory of dramatic art of Montreal. In the years I worked for Nicole, I saw her as my spiritual mother (during hard times with my mom). Our amazing relationship continues to this day, something I would never have imagined at the time.

After I finished at the Conservatory, I met Warren Robinson. Warren is a world-renowned acting coach who studied with two of the most influential acting instructors in modern history: Lee Strasberg of the Actor's Studio (The Method) and Stella Adler. Among his classmates were Paul Newman, James Dean, Jane Fonda, and Marilyn Monroe. In addition to teaching in New York City, he has worked all over the world, won prestigious awards, and been named among the best acting coaches in New York.

In the early 1990's, a student from Quebec suggested Warren come to Montreal. I took a master course with him four times a year for four years, and it was powerful. From Warren, I learned about being present in your acting so that the character's feelings and actions are real, not just a representation of reality. This is a difficult concept to explain but it profoundly changes the nature of your performance. In addition to showing us how to be different on stage, Warren also helped me build my self-confidence and see my hypersensitivity as a gift that allowed me to express myself to the fullest.

Warren was also the first person to have the guts to tell me that I was the victim of my own failure as an actress despite what he said was my tremendous talent. He forced me to confront my self-sabotaging behaviours and, as you have read, in many ways that was the beginning of my incredible and healing journey.

Another mentor, one precious to my heart, who became my best friend and my soul sister is Guylaine Grenier. As an accredited coach, psychosociologist and trainer she has given me the honour of walking and learning from her great teaching. Guylaine, for me, is not about raising the bar, she IS the bar (ha, ha, ha). I am moved by how she embodies a path of deep loyalty and integrity. Guylaine helps people think outside of the box. She also has an inherent sense of justice as she remains objective and neutral while teaching on a heart level. She definitely contributed to my being able to embody my strength and to see who I really am. Guylaine is also a new role model for me in terms of embodying the unknown to create a new path go beyond the evidence. Our 16-year partnership is a blessing for both of us, and we continue to develop new paths to help bring more awareness to the world. Guylaine is ahead of her time.

Napoleon Hill and My Mentors

Throughout this book you have read a lot of quotes by Napoleon Hill, so you can understand how studying his book transformed my way of thinking. Hill's principles are now at the foundation of all I do. They drive me to want to "lead a life of significance" and to continue to become a better teacher.

I have grown so much since beginning my business. The company's core values "serve as a compass for our actions and describe how we behave in the world." They are: Unity, Loyalty, Edification. Wow! What a code to live by.

I have had the great privilege of being a student of Raymond Aaron in his "Speaker Workshop" and I can only say, WOW. What an inspiration. What a humble, funny and powerful mentor he has become to me. I relate to his authenticity and the generous way he delivers so much value about the power of our words and the way to interact with others in need of bigger or greater assistance. I could see aspects of my own inner skills, the ones I already possess, but Raymond nailed it as he is the master! (ha, ha, ha), I love him so much! I love witnessing him and am delighted to be taught by Raymond. I understand why I was attracted to him at first sight. His heart is a gift, and his mastery in front of audiences is the embodiment of what a great speech is. I attended Raymond's writing program and I am so honoured to be a co-author with him.

Marcia Wieder is my spiritual wisdom teacher. With her, nothing has been left behind or unclothed. I am ever grateful for the lessons and healing I have received and all the love and integrity this powerful Dream Coach® has brought into my life. Marcia's brilliance and significance shine through every pore of her heart and soul. She is a real mentor to me in all aspects. Marcia is the example of what it means to be inspired. She embodies the Four Agreements, and is a master about speaking with impeccable words. I see myself in Marcia and I have great admiration for everything she creates with depth and wisdom. And, Marcia was right when she said our wound is our gift to the world.

Chapter 12

Conclusion

My journey has been a long but incredibly rewarding one, in which I had to take each step, one after the other. You will find this is true for you too. You don't just wake up one morning and find your life transformed. I've had many mentors and I have learned so much from each of them. I have taken seminars and courses and discovered something about myself in every one. Each time I gained wisdom from someone or something, it gave me the strength and willingness to accept the next lesson. Doing all this is how I have ignited my inner strength along the way.

So, what makes us who we are? It is a mystery to us when we live in the world without self-reflection and growth. But, when we allow ourselves to revisit the past, accept that we are wounded warriors, and begin to heal those wounds, we become enlightened. We can dig deep down and find the roots of the behaviours that no longer serve us. And, we can tug and tug at those roots as we step into our greatness.

When we learn through this process of discovery, we find that most of the problems we encounter when interacting with other people are grounded in the projections and behind-the-scenes work each participant in the conversation brings to the discussion. When we learn to really listen for what is actually being said, and take a moment to think before we speak, the outcome is extraordinarily different, and more productive to our mutual success. And, mutual success is the key to it all!

Live your life with integrity. Stand up for yourself with purpose and compassion for others. Accept people for who they are. If the people you are working with are not taking actions that benefit the entire group, it is better to walk away than it is to fight to be right.

How To Ignite Your Inner Strength

Now that you have read this book, let me ask you some questions:

- What is your vision; what will make you feel successful, happy and free?
- Where are you on your journey toward achieving your vision?
- What season are you in?
- What are the three things about yourself that you want to let go?
- Have you nurtured your heart, soul and body today? What will you do tomorrow?

I came into this world a passionate woman, born to inspire others, but it took me a long time to find my place as a leader. It took even more time to refine the way I communicate with others so that I could become an even better leader. Today, I know to put myself in the other person's place and understand what they have been through. I have a thicker skin and can respond appropriately, from a place of courage and self-esteem. And, I know when to fight, when to stand up for myself without confrontation, when to compromise, and when to walk away.

How Can I Help You?

If you are ready to move further along your path, and to do what needs to be done, I can help you to:

- Reconnect to your core self – heart, soul, and body – with my "Human Circles of Life" workshop.
- Track behaviours and stay aware of what is needed to access to your core essence and spiritual practices.
- Let go of false beliefs when you are stuck in place.
- Reach a new level of transformation and use tools and practices that enables and empower you to surrender during challenging times.
- Merge your behind-the-scenes learning with your present-day situation to raise yourself to a new level of transformation.
- Surrender to what comes and then come out on the other side of any difficulties.
- Move through your seasons with compassion for yourself and others, and then transition into a more productive, lighter season of growth and prosperity.
- Build better collaboration between team members and learn skills and strategies to help you or your business go to the next level.

Please remember that you don't need to go on your journey alone. While only you can take the actual steps, teachers and mentors can smooth the way and better prepare you to achieve your vision and live your goals.

I wish you only the best, dear reader, and many happy seasons of your life.

With love,

Dominique

If you would like to learn more about Dominique Lamy, her business, and her mentoring program or receive notices about any upcoming workshops and public speaking engagements, please visit www.IgniteYourInnerStrengthCoach.com.

To learn more about Dominique, the actress:

http://lesagentslibres.ca/artiste/dominique-lamy/

https://uda.ca/utilisateurs/482129

https://www.linkedin.com/in/dominique-lamy-7155b98/

Suggested Reading

- *Think and Grow Rich* by Napoleon Hill
- *Napoleon Hill's Keys to Success The 17 Principles of Personal Achievement* by Napoleon Hill
- *Your Right to Be Rich- Read by The Author* (CDs), by The Napoleon Hill Foundation
- *The Care of Soul* by Thomas Moore
- *The Alchemist* by Paulo Coelho
- *Listen to your Body* - Your Best Friend on Earth by Louise Bourbeau
- *Awakening Intuition: Using Your Mind-Body Network for Insight and Healing* by Mona Lisa Schulz
- *The Artist's Way, Spiritual Path to Higher Creativity's Way* by Julia Cameron
- *Kryon Series,* by Lee Carroll
- *Secrets of the Millionaire Mind* by T. Harv Eker
- *Business of the 21st Century* by Robert T. Kiyosaki
- *The Seven Spiritual Laws of Success* by Deepak Chopra
- *The Power of Now* by Eckhart Tolle
- *Body Self and Soul* by Jack Lee Rosenberg
- *The Four Agreements A Practical Guide to Personal Freedom* (Unabridged) by Don Miguel Ruiz (Audio)
- *Les Compagnons du devenir "16 coachs témoignent",* sous la direction de Danièle Darmouni; co-author, Guylaine Grenier
- *Les 7 clés du Leadership Féminin, Diriger avec la Tête et le Coeur* de Janie Duquette
- *Dear Lover a woman's guide to men, sex, and love's deepest bliss* by David Deida

How To Ignite Your Inner Strength

- *Rising Strong, The Reckoning. The Rumble. The Revolution. (Unabridged)* by Brené Brown (Audio)
- *The Power of Vulnerability : Teachings of Authenticity, Connection, and Courage* by Brené Brown
- *The Dark Side of the Light Chasers* (Unabridged) by Debbie Ford
- *Courage* by Debbie Ford
- *The Untethered Soul* by Michael A. Singer
- *The Surrender Experiment The Journey Beyond Yourself* (Unabridged) by Michael A. Singer
- *DREAM* by Marcia Wieder

Testimonials

"Dominique is a woman of endless curiosity about the essence and meaning of life. I met this wonderful actress in 1996. I hired her in a strategic program I created and together we trained in Quebec companies. During years of participation, Dominique has proven to be a remarkable tool for helping other people transcend the limits of human communication by being the "challenge" in exercises that promote openness to others. I have seen people pass into second states... from protection mode to having deep feelings about what is going on for them and for the other person. I always say that, with Dominique, they have the opportunity to cross the mirror and see the other person's unrecognized reality. Her talent is to take the right emotion and stay in discomfort in the name of the learning process for others. It is her gift. Being with her is never trivial! She knows how to indulge with all her generosity and intelligence, whether it is on stage or just sitting beside you on a bench. This precious friend gives birth today to a courageous life path that is so inspiring. Let yourself be accompanied by her words; they are true."

Guylaine Grenier
Psychosociologist, CRHA, Supervisor and Executive Coach - PCC,
Facilitator of Organizational Transformation - President - G2Consultants Inc. (Professional Coaching and Development)

"Dominique, a living force since she was very little, has always followed the impulses of her passions. Strong in her convictions, she never hesitated to take the unfrequented paths and to remain faithful to her deep aspirations. Dominique is an authentic and inspiring woman because of her ability to renew herself. I adore her for the truth she carries within herself but, above all, for her power to communicate and to shine."

Francine Lamy

"We had the privilege of presenting the business opportunity to Dominique, this fearsome and strong woman who carries within her the desire to surpass and to become a better version of herself. From the beginning, and through her learning, we felt that she was struggling with what had made her a victim in life; she was aware of it, but had to be confronted to transform her insecurities and turn into a confident woman. She has worked on how to stop pleasing other people first and how to be respected, despite her desire to be loved. We have observed her willingness to be out her comfort zone and face the situations that compelled her to take charge of her business and earn her right to financial and professional autonomy. Her commitment, going to conventions, programs, and workshops year after year has allowed us to witness her overcoming her relational challenges and rise to the rank of a great leader. We had the good fortune to laugh and cry with Dominique, who became a friend and a gift in our lives because of her qualities as a human being. We were able to hear this exceptional woman in several working contexts, including as an experienced coach, teaching and preaching loyalty by embodiment, knowing how to build up her working partners and friends (even those who have done her wrong), because she has this greatness of soul. The fruits of her harvest are the fruits of her seeds and we know that her story will inspire you and move you deeply as it has us. She will show you the importance of having tenacity while respecting who you really are because she has this admirable courage to go and reach beyond herself."

Michel Desjardins & Mélanie Gagnon
Professional Pianist Musician and Professional singer performer - Emerald Consultant

"Dominique is one of the great women in my life who inspires my steps on my path of expansion and growth. Dominique manifests ardor, passion, constancy, and perseverance. She shows us the way to surpass ourselves by preserving and nourishing respect and love of self. Dominique is a woman of words, trust, and heart. She enriches our existence on many levels."

Geneviève Sirois
Professional Herbalist, Practitioner in Trager Approach, Professor of Biodanza, Speaker

Testimonials

"I met Dominique Lamy when she introduced me to the products and business opportunity she represents. I found Dominique very convincing and funny, but especially very inspiring. So, I decided on the spot, that I wanted to team up with a passionate woman like her. We both had this desire to make a difference and help others to have a better life. It is in that context that I know Dominique, who wears several hats in that she is also an actress. She spent a lot of time working with me, training and accompanying me as I met all the new and sometimes frightening challenges that presented themselves. She was very available, and I could always count on her support and help. With the years that passed, I really saw Dominique rise to the rank of a great leader. She worked very hard, climbed the ladder step by step, stayed on course, believed in her dreams, and continued to progress despite low blows, betrayals, disappointments, and much more. Dominique is unique and she has a real gift for communication. Her message is filled with emotions that make people relate to her and want to follow her. In my opinion, Dominique embodies the active leader, who is 100% involved, meets new people, travels, and surrounds herself with hosts and mentors.

Dominique is persistent and she knows how to keep focus, even when it is extremely difficult. In the face of adversity, one has two choices: be an ostrich with your head in the sand or have the courage to face your fears and follow your heart and soul. Dominique is a great leader. She is never the ostrich."

Sophie-Kim Bazinet
Teacher

"Dominique, a woman whose charisma is undeniable, knows how to help others understand and communicate in a unique way. She clearly passes on her message and, given her generosity of heart, touches each individual very personally, in his inner core. She does this by sharing with us, so sincerely, her life and joys, pains, pitfalls, challenges, and even her inner conflicts. This enables us, the audience, to listen and to recognize our inner selves within the context of our own history. We are thus inspired to draw from our depths the forces we didn't know were there."

Sylvie Dubé
Administrative Assistant

"I had the chance to meet Dominique at a turning point in our respective lives. She had just bought her first home, which was possible because of the success she had achieved in network marketing in less than a year. On my side, I was looking for a business opportunity to get me out of the restoration industry, in which I no longer find happiness.

I attended one of Dominique's presentations learned about the company which allowed her to buy her home. I was really impressed by how easily she conveyed her emotions when talking about the challenges that she had faced in both her past and present experiences. In fact, I was won over by Dominique's authenticity. That night, I was sold. I recognized myself in her story. By joining her organization, I was able to begin my first entrepreneurial classes quickly, and I continued to take them with her for a period of two years.

Today, I can state that I am an accomplished entrepreneur, in huge part because of Dominique, who knew how to mentor me and how to pass on her passion for people. I recommend to anyone still looking for his place in life, to be inspired by her history. She is authentic, touching, and generous. She will teach you that, when you decide to learn from your past mistakes, perseverance allows you to reach the highest peaks of your imagination."

Loupin Gagné
Marketing Director - Leaders Factory

"Fire is a wonderful thing! It comforts the body, the heart and the soul. Who does not have memories of happy evenings of songs and gently roasted marshmallows around a camp fire? If not mastered, though, fire can also be a destructive force...When I met Dominique, let's just say that the flame she carried within her was, at the very least, intense... perhaps a little too much so. Over the years, I have seen this sensitive and highly intelligent woman learn to control and to tame her fire. From an unpredictable blaze, she was able to draw a quiet and reassuring force that now comforts and enlightens those who still seek a path in the dark. Thank you, Dominique! The world can only be a better place with leaders such as yourself in it. And may the fire that feeds you kindle a myriad of candles in a world that needs much more light and less darkness, or bush fires!"

Patrick Baby
Actor and Entrepreneur

Testimonials

"I am proud today to present to you the Dominique Lamy that I know. Dominique is passionate, authentic, a hard worker, persevering, and the seeker of meaning. These innate qualities are integral parts of her DNA and have made her an accomplished entrepreneur. The things she has learned from great teachers over the last decade, particularly from the teachings of Napoleon Hill, have marked her way of recreating herself while putting into practice a new way of seeing and living her life. All the paths she has taken have also led her to realize one of her dreams, which is "to write, and to be a proof of how to make the impossible become possible". This book makes a wonderful statement."

Catherine Jalbert
Coach, Numerologist, Dream Analyst and Author

"A woman of the heart, Dominique exudes a great power in term of leadership. She knows how to capture the essence of the beings she accompanies. It is an immense privilege to be so close to her. Each one of our meetings arouses in me reflections or questions that incite me to increase my inner transformation. She ignites my spark of life."

Mélissa Malboeuf
Author, Coach, Speaker

"I know Dominique for only few months, but I can affirm that she has helped me to transform my life. Dominique is a person of heart, with a great soul; she is an excellent coach who guides me to overcome and free myself from what I drag in vain. She is frank and direct, does not force anything, and respectively listens to my rhythm, always. I see her as a 'bomb' of great energy. In her presence, one can only grow and radiate."

Caroline Mayrand
Actress and Entrepreneur

"A few years ago, we met Dominique Lamy, who was brought into our business (by our friends and Emerald consultant, Michel Desjardins and Mélanie Gagnon). Dominique had some success as an actress, but she did not earn enough money to live on. I immediately discovered that Dominique has what is called "The Eye of the Tiger," the vision of a determined woman with drive to spare. She is a leader and, in her soul, 'a diamond raw to polish.' Every time we met with her, my wife and I thought it was surely she who would become the next Diamond on our team. She followed many courses and took tons of training and mentoring. She is very coachable, and has acquired all that it takes to become an example of how to assure success. Dominique is a woman of heart who loves people and wants the best for them. What a true leader and mentor she is. Read this book, and let yourself be inspired by this wonderful woman."

Ginette Bienvenue & Jean-Noël Sirois
Diamond Consultant

FREE OFFER

FOR a FREE copy of Dominique's *Wisdom of LOVE, Wisdom of MENTOR* please visit www.IgniteYourInnerStrengthCoach.com